THE ANSWERS WITHIN

Find Your Soul Purpose and Ignite Your Hidden Superpowers

SHARON KIRSTIN

ISBN: 978-3-00-056417-8

DOWNLOAD THE FREE WORKBOOK

www.sharonkirstin.com/bookbonus

IT'S MY GIFT TO YOU

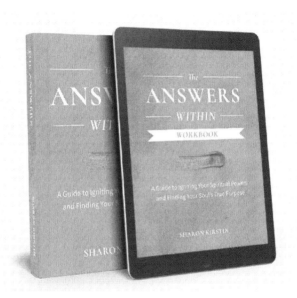

DON'T WAIT!

ALSO WATCH THE <u>FREE VIDEO TRAINING SERIES</u> NOW
AND SAY "YES" TO A LIFE OF PURPOSE AND POWER:

www.sharonkirstin.com/purpose

"*The meaning of life is contained in every single expression of life. It is present in the infinity of forms and phenomena that exist in all of creation.*"

— *Michael Jackson*

Table of Contents

To your biggest self

Introduction

What's the secret question you ask yourself when you're alone? The one that makes your stomach turn. The one you haven't asked out loud because the answer may be too painful? Three small words that have the potential to change your life in an instant...if you let them.

"Is this it?"

You're probably ambitious and successful in your job. You've worked your way up the corporate ladder or found your alternative path to what means success to you. The more your goals are being checked off your list, the less willing you are to sacrifice your health, time, and energy for a job you could get laid off from, if someone else decided. Maybe you also realize that more success (money, position, influence) takes up more and more of your life force the further you go. You just don't advance as easily as you did in the beginning of your career. Maybe you've even put life achievements that you've always wanted on the back burner — traveling the world, marriage, kids, or something else you dream of. There was just not enough time in the day to do it all.

So, now — just between you and me — how do you feel? Are you passionate about your life? Maybe you're hesitant to admit it. I know I was. Maybe you haven't dreamed freely in a long time or have lost touch with your innermost dreams and desires. Is there a chance (even just a slight one) that what you're so diligently working to achieve is only an outdated conditioning that yearns to be overhauled with fresh, empowering, fulfilling, and soulful goals that represent *your truth*?

I was thirty-one when I hit the corporate goal I set for myself. I was working as Director Shop and Mobile for a luxury fashion e-commerce company. In the years before, I had built an entire department for a fashion start-up from scratch, hiring over eighty employees in less than two years. I oversaw all the user experience decisions and strategy for mobile apps and website features. Everything to maximize user engagement and increase the amount purchased. It's not only that I had a great title and the six-figure income I always wanted, but I also had the opportunity to grow through the (good) challenges at work. Kind of an ideal scenario. But something clicked for me once I had the top position and the big income (my definition of success back then).

I wasn't happy. In fact, I felt more miserable than ever.

I decided to take my piling-up vacation days and travel far up into the Himalayan Mountains and meditate. It was on that meditation pillow that a thunderbolt of lightning (or so it felt to me) uplifted me from my meditation pillow and gave me a deep, spiritual insight that would change the whole trajectory of my life.

I traveled sixteen hours in a bus back to the New Delhi airport along steep stone cliffs that seemed like a metaphor for the act of balance I was moving toward. I would have to navigate a radical shift to be able to create the life I could love and enjoy living every single day.

Ever since, I have committed my days to being on purpose in my life and contribute to those around me. Not only have I reawakened my psychic gifts, my unique art of energy healing, and mastered my mindset, but most of all, I have found my truth. With it, life flows to me and happens *for* me.

Many of my coaching clients have experienced rapid, deep, and lasting transformations by implementing the how to's and working through the exercises I'm going to share with you in this book.

Ivonne, for instance, felt stuck in her corporate job and instead desired to share her knowledge with the world about nutrition for clear skin. Going through the processes I'll share with you in this book, she said, "Sharon helped me identify and release my fears and limiting beliefs. I knew I didn't live the life I wanted for myself, but also wasn't quite ready to take the leap and start my own business. I didn't feel good enough, capable enough, and I had big issues around money. Yet, within a couple of weeks, I went from believing that I didn't deserve money to fully clearing my debt. That I am free from all the worries within such a short period of time feels like magic to me!"

Heena was already very successful in her business, but felt called to create a purposeful business that would serve her heart's desires. "Sharon guided me to realize my superpower, and we determined the key pillars in my business. Following her manifesting process, I could prove to myself that thoughts followed by action really do create specific outcomes."

If you are an ambitious person with a spiritual nag (hey, chanting Om Shanti at the end of yoga class feels kinda good) and feel deep (maybe subtle) longing to unravel the mysteries of life, then this book was written as a lighthouse of guidance for you.

My promise to you is that this book will change your perspective on life. You'll see life, the Universe, and yourself as you never did before. You'll be initiated into the circle of ascension activists who carry the light. It's been written in the most powerful, high-vibration I have ever experienced. The words kept flying out onto paper, and I was amazed at the wisdom pouring through me. Yes, my name is on the cover, but this book feels to me, quite frankly, as if it came from a different dimension as a gift to you.

I have been given visions of you reading the book. With every word, every sentence read, your energy begins to shift; it ascends, and you transform more and more into the powerful cocreator that you are in Divine truth. I saw you, thought the sole act of reading this book, reattune to your soul essence and purpose. I hope you'll feel the magic.

If you are still reading, you've found this book for a reason. Even more likely, it has found you.

Don't be the person who disregards her Divine guidance. The Universe tries to reach you and show you a path. Maybe you have asked a question, prayed, or are trying to find the next step in your life.

Listen to your soul, your guidance and your intuition — could it be that Divine timing is at play and you're ready to live your full truth? Is now the time to answer your soul's call for a more fulfilled and on-purpose life? A journey of a thousand miles begins with the first step. This book can open you up to a more purposeful, magical, and fulfilled life. Take the first step.

> *"I would rather be hated for who I am,*
> *than loved for who I'm not."*
> *– Kurt Cobain*

CHAPTER 1

OPEN YOUR MIND

"The mass of men lead lives of quiet desperation."
– Henry David Thoreau

Zombies in Neverland

What is the one thing you can't get more of, no matter how big the money bundle you throw on the table? What's the one thing that we all, rich and poor, have the same amount of? The ticking in the background of our life that lets us hurry through our days. Time.

In a world that's getting more and more fast-paced, time becomes the most valuable resource. Whatever we do, we just can't get more hours in a day. So instead, we try to squeeze more and more into the twenty-four hours at hand. We optimize, we hurry, we stress, we make plans, we are constantly thinking of what's next on the list.

In a world that's becoming smaller and faster with all the information constantly pushed through to our mobile devices and the instant connections we can make through the internet, the statement most of us recite in our minds for the better part of our waking time is, "I need more hours in the day." Or maybe the remixes, "If only I had more time," "I don't have time," or "When I have time" (code for: never). It's a chronic disease of stress that spreads like a wildfire. Technical advances held to sparkling promises of relief and wealth for the masses, but all they seem to do is enslave us more. It makes the use of our time so much more productive, which is supposed to be a good thing and alleviate us from repetitive work. But what do the increasing abilities to increase our performance really do to our mind, body, and soul? Our bodies are stressed and get sick, our minds are overloaded with impulses, we seek refuge in meditation and practice yoga just to stay sane, our souls are dying under the weight of expectations and performance imposed on us.

The workforce is a different place than it was back when our parents started jobs. Computers were novelties, and people would actually send letters through "snail mail." Can you believe it? Just recently I was decluttering my bookshelf and found *The Oxford Dictionary of English*. I must have kept it from around twenty years ago when I was in school. Needless to say, I donated it. Who needs a physical dictionary nowadays? My best guess: nobody. We go online and with two clicks, get countless websites with free translation services. Crazy efficient and convenient world...

I was sitting in my Mom's basement at age fifteen listening to the whistling sounds of the modem. I was staring at it intensely with eyes wide open, my body in excited attention, and fingers crossed that this time it would connect me to the endless space that is the World Wide Web. It didn't always work, you know. Websites had bad user experiences (maybe one of the reasons I ended up in website optimization later on in my corporate career), there was no Google (can you imagine?!), and people would never in a million years enter their credit card online. We've come a long way from spending all our pocket money on chatting with new online friends via ICQ to flat-rates with ultra-fast optical fiber cables to transfer the ever-increasing demands of data volume. It's also a long way from that basement with the malfunctioning modem to having free Wi-Fi access in almost all public places.

We are always connected, always "on," aren't we? After all, you may miss that uber important picture of your friend Stacy's healthy kale salad for lunch that's being pushed to your attention from social media. Let's be honest, not all information we're exposed to is helpful, nurturing, or even supportive to us. More is not better. But with bigger amounts of information constantly thrown at our attention, it becomes increasingly difficult to dissect what is truly helpful and supportive to us.

Did you know that our will and decision power is a finite resource? It diminishes throughout the day, the more decisions we make. Ad commercials alone waste a lot of our willpower. The decisions not to buy, not to look, not to react, are also decisions. Advertising statistics say that we are exposed to 5,000+ ads per day. Now I would say that depends on where you live and how you spend your day, but the fact is, marketers have products and they fight over your attention to make the sale. We're not only rushing through life, trying to keep up with the demands of our jobs, but we're also bombarded with conditioning that tells us what we should and shouldn't want. Sounds like a challenging time to be alive and even more challenging to stay true to yourself. Designing a life that recharges you instead of drains you from any willpower and energy you have left over becomes a dream that you'll attend to "when you have time."

How do you feel? Do you feel like you need to find your place and own it? Like a dog marking its territory to state you "made it" and you'll stay put. We constantly have to prove where we stand. Competition seems to be the big word that drives us past our strength reserves and into burnout. After all, there are at least five more people around the corner who could do our job. And there is always this one person in the office that wants your job and is just waiting for you to slip. Nowadays, it's not about finding your place and living there comfortably. No; you need to defend it constantly from the hungry flock of vultures circling you with envious eyes.

Yet, the never-ending competition and increasingly destructive workplaces are maybe (just maybe) not the worst part of it all. As humans, we can project into the future and anticipate a likely outcome based on our own experience or experience from others that has been shared with us. We're able to see where actions may lead us in the long run. Super valuable in so many different scenarios to prevent us from harm and death. But it can also be a tool of transformation. There's an outer journey you're walking, and it may lead you to a great job position, high income, standing in society, whatever your goals are. And then there's your inner journey. The inner journey will determine your happiness and fulfillment with all the outer achievements. Are your journeys aligned or are they drifting apart? Is what you're creating on the outside a reflection of your *true* inner desires?

My moment of truth came when I found myself asking, "Will I keep going like this for the next forty years?" "Will I have the energy to keep up?" "What is all this *really* good for?" Did you also ever wonder where you're heading in your life? Did you ever think back at how much it took you to get to where you are? The long hours, missed travels, neglected friends, the lost partnerships. What for? To keep pushing toward goals that make you happy for a minute and then you have to find a new glorified goal to achieve?

Is this it?! Is this what life is about?!

Let's wrap this puppy up. Most likely, you have a really nice job and you outperform your colleagues. You are stressing each day to meet all your appointments and deadlines on time (there is only so much time available in the day), while you are drained from your willpower minute by minute (there is only so much available as well). You find it difficult to recharge your batteries so you've probably included some form of meditation or yoga into your week to keep your act together. Maybe you've picked up one or two bad habits along the way that stick like glue because, let's face it, they give you release. Yet, they keep draining you and make you feel weak (I've been there). You try to find happiness in the next shiny thing you buy or the next big achievement, but satisfaction wears off leaving you feeling a bit more empty each time. To top this bowl of deliciousness off with a bright red cherry: all this effort and energy flows into your work, but you feel like you aren't making a big difference. Are you really helping a cause that's close to your heart? Will somebody say that your life's work inspired and helped them? Or will you just fade from the planet without leaving a meaningful mark, without anybody remembering you for what really matters: *the love you shared.*

You're smart, so you looked around at other people. You noticed that everyone is living this way and more or less convinced yourself that it's okay. Life is hard. Or maybe something is wrong with *you* that you feel different. So you try harder to follow the herd and fit into the stereotyped images of achievement. "It can't be so wrong — it seems to be working for others. Probably I'm just doing it wrong." Or...not? Here's the key question: why did you pick up this book? Really take a moment now, breathe, and let your answer surface to your awareness. I'll give you my five cents on this in a moment. Really...do it now. Why did you pick up this book?

Okay, got your answer? Here's my best guess and you correct me if I'm wrong: You picked up this book because you're different than the crowd — and you're starting to *feel* it.

You're not one of the lemmings jumping off the cliff. You're beginning to see that the system you're part of is faulty and so many are just sugarcoating their lives with a sprinkle of glam. *Looking* happy is way more important than *being* happy. Although everybody acts as if they have their act together and are riding the rainbow wave to Neverland — my lingo to say "happy." They really don't, and they really aren't happy when you look behind the masks. People disguise their frustration, pain, and disillusionment with life. They numb themselves with entertainment, addictions, and work. They try so hard to patch up their wounds, but the band-aids are torn, the bandages are hanging loose, and the wounds are dripping blood. They act as if everything is okay while they're walking around like zombies.

But you, my dear, are *different*.

You are ready to…

- morph into your biggest, most beautiful and powerful version of yourself
- alter the course of your life to make it a masterpiece that you'll be proud of
- question the validity of the rules society wants to impose on you
- open your mind to a different way of life, thinking, and even being
- reconnect with your soul essence and the true creator powers within you

Travel with me on the journey through this book and I'll initiate you into a whole new way of being, seeing, and living life. It will be life changing. Am I making too much of a promise here? "A course in miracles" defines a miracle as a shift in perspective. This book is filled with new concepts. So I trust you're ready for some mind-bending, shifts in perspective, and miracles. After all, your soul brought you here. Right now, to this very moment, in which you can change the trajectory of your life forever.

> *"Living up to an image that you have of yourself or that other people have of you is inauthentic living."*
> *— Eckhart Tolle*

Van Gogh's Internet

Now that I've painted a picture of gloom and doom, here's the truth: there are always two sides of a coin and reality is never objective. It is what you believe to be true about reality that will determine your emotions, actions, and achievements. From now on, we'll ride the waves of high vibes together. So, I have good news: times aren't only getting faster, but also humankind is getting more conscious. That's why you're reading this. Consciousness is the currency of the new earth.

New earth? Don't worry; I'm not sending you off on a spaceship with a mission to populate a planet far, far away (yes, I love Science Fiction). You'll stay right here on Mother Earth because *this* is where the magic happens. In the past years, an avalanche of consciousness has started rolling and with it, the vibration of the planet continues to rise. Planet Earth is ascending into a higher dimension of existence and you're on this once-in-a-lifetime ride with her. If this doesn't make sense to you right now, it's okay. Your head will never understand. But your heart does.

Your heart and soul have led you on a quest to find more purpose in your life. To stand for something you believe in and make a difference in the lives of others. Right now, you may not know how, what, and when. But any journey starts with the very first step in the right direction. You can fully trust the process I'm laying out for you here. I'm preparing your mind and soul to assimilate the information and transformation that will come through the teachings in this book. Have faith. Just take my word for it, for now.

I told you it would challenge what you "know." So, still feeling this book? You can drop off and stay put in your old ways anytime you like. No hard feelings. This really isn't for everyone. Or it may not yet be the right time. Your ego will try to stop you. Put the ego on mute. Read this book with your heart, not your mind.

Your soul is pushing you to investigate what you're created for. Why have you been put on this planet? Is there some talent you have that would benefit others? How can you live a life that fulfills you? A life of freedom, abundance, and happiness? They say, "Do what you love, and you'll never work a day." Maybe that's what you're looking for? I get it and I fully support you. We're becoming more conscious and starting to wake up from our sleepwalking state. We ask for the purpose of our life.

The generation of our grandparents was forced to build a life from the ground up. Their focus was to survive. They were hard workers, savers, and more often than not, they lived through a war. The generation of our parents grew up in peace and were able to thrive economically and push past survival into comfort.

Now our generation is blessed and cursed. Blessed because we grew up in a wealthy society (I'm assuming you grew up in a western civilized country), and we get to ask, "What's the purpose of life? Why am I here?" Only when all our basic needs (food, shelter, etc.) are met are we able to attend to our spiritual needs. The need for self-actualization. It's such a huge gift that we live in a time where we not only have the resources to discover our soul's gifts, but also the means to make a living from them.

The invention of the internet gives us vast opportunities to do business online, to spread our message, and to sell what we believe will make the world a better place. Artists can share their work to a massive audience compared to just decades ago. Just imagine what would've happened if van Gogh had lived in the era of the internet. Maybe his work would've gone viral while he was still alive.

Creatives no longer have to be starving artists, acknowledged for their accomplishments only after they die. Trainers and teachers can reach audiences in a personal way through videos and teach their tush off without any limits to the impact they can make. Hundreds, thousands, millions of people's lives improved by *one person*. And it's not a president or famous person. It's just the person next door making a living from home or location independent using the connectedness through the web. Freedom. Influence. The good life. Just think what you could achieve when you plug the two together: purpose + reach. Real change, real impact.

There's just one curse that comes with the luxury of having the opportunity to self-actualize, to find our purpose in life: *we don't know how*. Often we grew up with zero role models in our family. We couldn't learn from our grandparents or our parents. They've never learned how to do it themselves. Their generations were focused on a different set of rules, values, and goals.

It's up to you and me to take mankind to yet the next level. You're reading this right now because you are part of the purpose pack. We're running together like wolves howling in a new era of existence. A world in which we do not only survive, where we do not only play, but where we thrive into our full creator powers with intention, stamina, and vision beyond ourselves. The dark ages of separation are over; a time of conscious connection has begun.

Isn't this exhilarating and exciting? Just imagine what the next generation will be able to create when we lay this foundation! Are you with me on finding your purpose and unleashing your full potential? Yep? ...thought so.

"If I am what I have and if I lose what I have,
who then am I?"
– Erich Fromm

Promises, Regrets and Success

Bronnie Ware, a palliative nurse, recorded the top five regrets of her dying patients and shared them in her book. The #1 regret that she heard was: "I wish I'd had the courage to live a life true to myself, not the life others expected of me."

Boom. If you weren't sitting, I bet you are now. It's worth reading it again. Let it marinate your emotional body.

Project yourself into the future again — this time with a twist (and lemon zest). What would you regret *not* having done when you're about to die?

Maybe you regret the times when fear held you back of taking risks. The time you didn't say "I love you," because the other person may not say it back. The time you didn't go talk to the hunk at the bar because you may be rejected (but he could well be your husband by now). The time you didn't speak up for your needs because you may be viewed as "difficult." The time you didn't follow the inkling in your heart that sang of purpose and passion because you may fail.

With this type of resumé, the ever-daunting question, "Am I all I can be?" will haunt us for the rest of our life.

The truth is that you have already failed if you don't follow a heart that calls out to you. You failed without ever taking action. The feeling of failure and resentment will wrap its grip around your heart. In every quiet moment, it will whisper a tale of "could haves" and "should haves" in your ear that will leave your soul bitter and brittle dried up like a furrowed desert.

The truth is that whatever is in your heart and soul, you *can* do it. It's there for a reason. And the reason is that you are the *only* one who can bring it forth in your unique way. It may have been done before. But it hasn't been done *your* way. When I talk to my clients, this is a theme that I see over and over again. "It's already been done. Why bother. Nobody needs another xyz. My creative work won't add value." I beg to differ. While there is only so much new under the sun after thousands of years of civilization, the crucial ingredient that will make your work unique is...drumroll please: You.

Imagine a big buffet with all kinds of salad. People love salad so they check out the buffet. They scout around the table and choose the one that they like best. Why do they like one more than the other? It's all salad. Well maybe the dressing is different, or the ingredients, or the way it's presented. The same goes for your work, gifts, and creative expression. Others may be out there doing the same thing, but they do it in their style, their voice, for their audience. You may have the same message, but by being who you are and by saying it your way, you can suddenly help a completely different audience.

"Competition," by the way, is a good thing. It shows there is a market for your work, service, or offer. So, don't let that be your excuse why don't pursue your dreams. I say "competition" in quotation marks, because on the creative plane, where we operate from now on (pinky swear?), there is enough for everyone. Competition does not exist. The Universe is limitless and can take care of all of us in never-ending showers of abundance.

I don't know you personally (yet), but I believe you are already a quite successful person, probably you're really ambitious in your life, and have high standards. Success is what drives you to grow above and beyond your limits. Maybe you're even proud of how you were able to surpass others on the corporate ladder. This is all great and I admire you for that. I also admire you for everything else you've done, even if I was completely and utterly wrong with my assumption before. (Then you've probably been a seeker all your life for what success would be worth fighting for.) Either way, I assume you've had your share of success in life and business. The types of achievements that others looked at with big glazing eyes of admiration. I hate to break it to you, but I have to:

"Success without fulfillment is the *ultimate* failure."

It's a quote from one of my favorite mentors, Tony Robbins. It stuck with me like glue. Think about it. Where does success without meaning lead? You feel more and more hollow with every success you drive home. You believe more and more that something must be inherently wrong with you because other people seem to be happy with it. But you're not. You start to wonder, why society preaches us to do, be and, achieve these things. Notice the faulty system at work? The old system doesn't work anymore. Not for you, not for me, and not for many other soul seekers across the globe. You're not alone.

> *"We are here to awaken from the illusion of separateness."*
> *— Thich Nhat Hanh*

Expressing your Soul Essence

A new approach to work and basically to life is needed. The system that teaches children to sit in chairs all day, memorizing information, and imprinting monotonous tasks on them needs an upgrade. What's the point? So that they can go work in jobs as adults that are just as uninspiring? This system worked well a hundred years ago when the industry needed factory workers who would do repetitive tasks in one spot all day. But nowadays, that's no longer what we need or desire. An evolution is taking place where humankind is progressing into a new era of life. Work is no longer separate from who we are. Companies took a step toward increasing work-life balance when they saw that employees were burning out. Yet, it's also only a patch on the wound.

The new approach is to see human beings as who they truly are: a multilayered expression of the essence of life. You are not a body. You are also not only a mind or a soul. You are all that in one. The expression of yourself moves through all your levels of being and seeks to find authentic expression in all you do. Your essence is within your soul. Your soul holds so much more wisdom, experience, and energy than your human mind can understand. Beyond the three-dimensional life we experience on planet earth, lie dimensions of higher existence that are hard to fathom with a human brain. Yet, your heart can. Your heart always knows the truth and can sense the truth. You hear truth when your heart suddenly expands and for no logical reason at all, it feels like coming home to truth that you once knew. No matter whether the brain can make full sense of it. Some people call it a gut feeling, others instinct or intuition. It is the part in you that constantly communicates with its essence or source.

The source of who you are, that your soul is part of, is one all-encompassing energy of love. There are different names for the essence of life as well — God, the Universe, Source Energy, the Supreme, the Divine, the All Mind, Infinite Intelligence. All names for the One.

Do you feel the yearning for reconnection? To be part of something bigger than you are? That's because your soul essence knows you *ARE* more than what you currently believe you are. It's guiding you to remember your truth, your power, and potential. This longing of your soul to help you rediscover who you are in (Divine) truth guided you to pick up this book. It pushes you forward to discover your strengths, talents, and purpose. This primal force in you desires nothing more than for you to be in your biggest, fullest expression. It cannot act or desire differently because it lives through you. Source energy expresses itself in and through you. The more you live your truth, the more you contribute to life. And *this* is what we need to learn now, so that we can pass it on to the next generation. Scarcity and restraint are not holy. They are resistance to the force of life that wants to express itself through you. By dimming your light and making yourself small, you are *not* helping anyone.

> *"Our deepest fear is not that we are inadequate. Our deepest*
> *fear is that we are powerful beyond measure. It is our light,*
> *not our darkness that most frightens us."*
> – *Marianne Williamson*

There are only two forces in life: creation and destruction. Think about it. You can not do or be both at the same time. Just like night and day will never happen at the same time. Either you are growing into a bigger expression of who you are or you are resisting and with it, destroying life, even if it may be your own.

Game Time

A fish is unaware of the nourishing water it's frolicking in. Unless...you take it away, right? Only on land will it realize that its most natural state of being is swimming in water. It realizes something is off, it can't breathe, it feels tremendous discomfort. It's then, and only then, that it will try to find its way back into its essence.

The same goes for us humans. Our essence is pure love, source energy. But being in this blissful state, in whatever form that may be, will not let us understand what it truly means to be 100 percent love. Does this make sense?

The daylight has no meaning without the night. Above has no meaning without a below. Light has no meaning without darkness. We understand this world and ourselves through duality.

Our three-dimensional world allows us an experience of duality and with it the illusionary experience of separation from our source and each other. So, how would the Supreme create a scenario in which it can realize its true self? How can unconditional, all-encompassing Divine love, pure existence, find self-actualization?

I'll keep this as simple as possible, because it may well be that this is the first time you are exposed to this concept. Let me paint a picture for you, for the sake of simplicity and clarity. I'll explain the setup of earth life and why you chose to be here...and for fun's sake, I'll use and slightly adapt the rhymes of The Fresh Prince, Will Smith.

Now this is a story all about how
My life got flipped, turned upside down
And I'd like to take a minute
Just sit right there
I'll tell you how I became the princess of a planet called earth

In source energy born and raised
Dwelling in love was how I spent most of my days
Chillin' out maxin' relaxin' all cool
And supporting souls in dimensions outside of my pool
When a couple of guys who were up to real good
Started cranking up a whole new type a' hood
This one little idea burned in us like mad
We said, "Let's move in on earth and self-actualize there."

Others were curious and begged day after day
So we packed 'em up and brought 'em along the way
We blew a kiss and then we got our ticket
With open hearts we said "We might as well kick it."

First class, yo, when I'll be born
I hear that all my memory'll be gone
Is this how the incarnated people living like?
Hmm, k I'll make it alright.

But wait I hear we'll be alone, scared, all that
Is this the type of place that we just sent this cool cat?
I don't think so
I'll see when I get there
I hope they're prepared for the princess on earth

Well, my soul landed and when I came out
There were random people, my memory's wiped,
even my name's out
I need to learn everything from scratch
I just got here
I match with the quickness like lightning, conformed

I whistled along and what I learned is clear
The mind has the power and fear executes here
If anything I could say that this life was rare
But I thought, "Nah, forget it.
— I'm home in this flair."

The years go by and I'm now about 78
Weary of struggle, I yell out, "What's this 'bout here?"
Boom, my body dies
I'm love 'n' back in source energy, yo
Now I recall why I went, damn, now let's go try again!

Okay, okay, if this didn't hit home yet (although I'm sure the tune of *The Fresh Prince of Bel Air* is playing in your head right now), let me find yet another way of explaining.

Once upon a time in a dimension much more ethereal, you, me, and many other expressions of source (souls) had a realization. We were happy and content, being one with unconditional love and light. Just like the fish in the water, we couldn't understand what this meant because all we ever knew was love. Let's say we started brainstorming on how we could realize who we really are.

So, you started off with a great idea: "Hey, let's play a game! What if we forgot that we are pure love and light? When we remember it will be like waking from an illusion or dream!"

And I responded: "Intriguing! But we would have to wipe all memory of our time here so that we believe only what we see with our physical eyes. It would be the ultimate illusion — radical separation from our source. Otherwise it won't work. We won't believe the illusion."

You again: "Yes! If we believe we are separated from our source, this would be the perfect environment to be able to remember who we really are!"

Jumping with excitement I counter: "Right. But that sounds a bit too easy. How about we create an instrument, let's call it the ego, that will constantly feed us with fear. Its job would be to point out why it's not safe to follow our heart and reconnect with source. It could also create an additional layer of illusion so that we try to find reasoning in everything that happens and whatever conclusions we draw, we believe them to be real. That'll make it a real challenge to embark on that journey of self-actualization and remember our essence!"

You: "Oooh, I'm excited! How about we top it off with an environment full of potential risks, distractions, and shiny things that the ego wants to engage with?"

Me: "Love it! And we would have to believe that if our body dies that's it, right? So that we strive for survival and are really distracted from our main goal of reconnection with our essence."

You: "I know just the place! Let's go to this shiny, beautiful blue planet in the third dimension. It's terrific!"

You and me, we agreed to play a fun game called earth life. On a soul level, we decided that we wanted to be part of this unique experience. Especially during this transformational time of awakening and ascension into higher dimensions of consciousness. Many people are already having experiences of true self-realization and with it they raise the vibration of the planet for us all. How exhilarating!

When we signed up for this journey, we knew what this game was about. We were excited to get this exclusive opportunity of a physical body and free will. We knew what lessons we wanted to learn. What struggles we wanted to live through and master. What purposeful mission our life would hold for us and the whole planet. As part of the deal, we would have to forget everything, though, when we arrive on the other side of the veil in the 3D world. Otherwise you can't play. You'd know you're dreaming and with that, you'd wake up.

It's similar to the way they portrayed the dreams in the movie *Inception*. The subconscious of the dream architect is looking for the dreamer who provides the consciousness for the dream. Yet, the dream architect subconsciously knows that something is off because what he's seeing is not his truth. His subconscious senses that it's an illusion and from the moment the dream begins, it's on a quest to get rid of the dreamer so that it can realign with its truth, its essence.

In our 3D game, we're sleepwalking. Part of us knows it's a dream. Intuitively we begin searching for our truth, purpose, and connection. Yet, our memory is wiped, so we're not sure what we're looking for. Something just seems really off. We're walking around scratching our heads feeling like we just took a hard punch that left us feeling dizzy. We're disoriented and are desperately searching for a rope that'll save us from drowning.

Some of us are here to enjoy the game and others are called to transcend the game. Those who are ready to wake up from the dream and reconnect with their soul essence will guide us collectively into a new state of being. They will understand what the game was about: We descended from a higher consciousness into the third dimension, so that we can awaken to our Divine essence and deliberately reascend into a higher dimension of consciousness. The game is one of descension and reascension.

We descended into the third dimension to self-realize. We're on a mission to understand that we are not our bodies or minds. Our souls are flawless, pure Divine essence that chose to incarnate into a 3D body at this time and space. The illusion of the game is that we are separated from source. Separated from each other and from everything around us. How could you play the game without fully believing in it and sticking to its rules? There are physical rules set for this dimension, but what if you could harness your source powers by remembering who you *REALLY* are? Then you could draw upon the powers of creation to flow through life as a master. You'd transcend your pain of separation and become one with all that is. You'd leave behind the concept that anything in life ever happened *to* you, and instead understand that everything is happening *for* you.

You are Divine essence choosing a three-dimensional experience. Here you have the opportunity to remember that separation is only an illusion. You can dissolve the illusion by shining the light of awareness on your three-dimensional beliefs, habits, and fears. In awareness they can not prevail, and you are free to live your truth and full potential.

Once you're aware that you're playing the game, it becomes less serious. Many of us don't acknowledge that we all get out of the game the same way: death. We will die. Some sooner, some later. Many are so earnest, rigid, and fearful in what they do, as if they could win or lose or somehow cheat death. They can't. Accepting that this game is played one life at a time can completely shift the way you approach life. Your true self, your soul, is eternal.

Seeing yourself as a soul having a human experience, can change your perspective on life. You soften your grip, flow through life with ease, and trust in the guidance you receive. You remember that you are perfectly held with love, light, and support in this Universe. You can have faith in the mission you set out to accomplish during this lifetime. And yes, the mere fact that you are holding this book in your hands means that you *have* a mission, a Divine role to play, that will contribute to the ascension of the whole planet. You are here to raise others to higher grounds and support Mother Earth in her ascension process as well. You are important. You are needed. Your soul is sending you signs that it's time to make your move. Your soul already knows its purpose. And it's helping you to remember. You'll know soon.

Arguing with Reality

This essence within you, transcends your personality, your environment, and your dreams. This essence creates galaxies, stars, our planet, and you. It's the Divine source of all being. There is no difference between you and a star being born on the other end of the galaxy. It is birthed from the same substance, an infinite intelligence, that you are made of, and it has the same elemental purpose that you have: to expand and grow.

You surely expand and grow differently than a star, a tree, a flower, or an animal. Your privilege and opportunity as a thinking, self-aware being is that you can play this game of illusion. Your intellect and mind are perfectly suited to create the illusion of separation from source. You dwell in the past and worry about the future. You are hardly ever in the present moment fully focused on the now. Ironic, because the now is the only point in time where all of life happens. A dog, tree, planet, and even a child can't project into past or future. They are always in the now. Always present with what is. Never judging, arguing, reminiscing, or worrying. Adults are the only ones arguing with reality, dwelling on memories of the past, and projecting worry onto the future.

> *"Every time I argue with reality, I lose."*
> *— Byron Katie*

The crux is that you just can't win. If you argue with what is, it simply won't change your current experience. Feeling miserable about it, won't change it. It will only create more of what you don't want. Arguing with the present moment and its perceived malice, puts you in the position of a victim. You unconsciously create over and over again what you don't want more of.

Shifting Perspective

You're not the victim though. You are the creator of your reality. Remember that you are made of the same essence that creates worlds? That's who you *truly* are. You are part of that elemental force. Your feeling of separation and victimhood is only an illusion. You can never be separated from that which you are made of.

This also means that you are never separated from the tremendous powers of creation. They are flowing within you and through you at all times. You can draw upon them whenever you choose. That's why you are powerful beyond measure. It can be a bit scary to admit that to yourself because it means that you are fully responsible for everything in your life. *Everything.* You are never a victim.

Soul contracts have been made and fulfilled for you to have certain experiences that will trigger your growth and expansion. On a soul level, you have decided to be born into certain circumstances for the same reasons of growth.

Your energy attracts experiences, things, and people into your life on a daily basis. Your energy is colored by your beliefs, your habits, and emotions. That's why you have a unique experience of reality. You attract what matches your view of the world. This gives you endless power: by changing your beliefs, you can change your whole reality, your complete life! It puts all power back into your own hands. You can stop giving your power away to others through blame, victimhood, or playing small. It is you who can change *your* world.

Your biggest power lies in changing yourself. When you align your beliefs and emotions with the reality you desire, your actions automatically follow suit. You manifest from thought form into physical reality.

Usually our mind will try to dismiss empowering concepts like these. So maybe you're thinking, "Sounds good, but you can't change the world you live in. You can't change who's being elected as president or stop a war." That's true. Your power as a creator of *your* reality does not lie in changing other people. Your power lies in changing how *you* see and experience the world.

> *"If you change the way you look at things,*
> *the things you look at change."*
> – Dr. Wayne Dyer

The way you see, judge, and interact with the world around you is solely based on your belief system and conditioning. Your experience of the world is very different from the experience of the world from everyone else. You have a unique set of beliefs that act as filters. These filters color the perception of your reality. Your world view is unique and feeds into your Divine life purpose.

"Loving people live in a loving world.
Hostile people live in a hostile world.
Same world."
– Dr. Wayne Dyer

Elephants and Demons

What does it take to live a purposeful life? How can fulfillment, happiness, and abundance radiate from every cell of your being? Why is it so hard to take charge of our life and access our full potential? What do the people who succeed do differently than those who fail?

Demons.

They sneak up on you when you least expect them. You know who they are, because they have been lurking in the shadows your whole life. By now you're used to them being around. You have arranged your way around them. You don't even notice them consciously anymore. They're waiting in the dark alley that you won't dare walk down. You're too scared to confront this potent enemy. So they reign over you. Silently. From the shadows. They don't even have to speak up. Their sole presence and threats of pain are so daunting that you don't stand up to them. You avoid them like the plague, just like you avoid the dark alley. You lost once, maybe when you were a child or adolescent. You may have been pushed down the alley and met them. It hurt; that pain was unbearable, death-like. It made you believe that you're powerless. If you want to survive, you better comply with the demon's demands. But its rule is merciless and it will suck the life out of you. If you let it...

Have you ever heard why grown elephants can be kept captive with a small wooden plug in the ground? Elephants are the largest animals on the planet. Why would a 15,000-pound animal be imprisoned by a small plug superficially pounded into the ground? It's ridiculous, isn't it? Well, the elephant, let's call him Bimbo, hasn't always been a majestic giant. Bimbo was a baby elephant once. Back then, he tugged for hours and days, maybe weeks, to release the stake from the ground. He tried to break free countless times. He tried everything in his power to break loose and storm off into a life of freedom and power. But Bimbo wasn't strong enough. The small stake was strong enough to hold him captive. As the weeks went by, baby Bimbo gave up. His inevitable conclusion was that he wasn't strong enough to break free. The grip of the stake was strong. It could not be defeated.

Now you may say, okay, but Bimbo is grown now — he is strong enough *now*! He could easily pull it out and run free. Smart thinking. The thing is, Bimbo never tried again. What he learned as a baby, "I am not strong enough to break free," was ingrained as truth in his psyche. The belief became his reality, his identity. And as long as Bimbo doesn't question it and try again, he will stay a prisoner forever. It is crazy to think that it's so easy to keep such a powerful animal like Bimbo completely cut off from his true power with so little effort.

You were a child once, too. You, like all of us, got conditioned with your load of limiting beliefs and painful experiences that still keep a tight grip on you. These are the demons that keep you cut off from all that you can be, your full Divine potential. The demons' tool is *fear*. Nothing more and nothing less. They keep you believing that you're not strong, smart, or good enough to live your best life. The demons voices say, "Who do you think you are to reach for greatness?" "You don't deserve the good life." "You're full of yourself." "People will hate you." So you stick to what you know, put your head down, and keep going with the herd. Thanks demons...

We all get imprinted with beliefs from our family, friends, teachers, the media, and other influencers. Just like baby elephant Bimbo, you challenged your boundaries when you were young; you won, you lost, you got hurt. Some experiences were more traumatic than others and left their mark. Beliefs stick like glue, if we hear them often enough. Bonus points if they are charged with emotion, the super glue of beliefs.

You are the sum of your experiences plus the conclusions you have drawn from them about who you are. They have become your identity. Your belief system steers you every single day of your life. You think you're making decisions in your life, but it's not you who chooses. If you're not fully self-aware and conscious of your motives, you're acting based on your past experiences and what you *believe* to be true about yourself. Basically your three-year-old self is making all the decisions for you because you still follow the unquestioned belief patterns that were instilled in your subconscious when you were young.

The first characteristic of people living their purpose is self-empowerment. They do not allow their subconscious beliefs and conditioning to steer them into a direction they aren't willing to go. They are courageously facing fear, limiting beliefs, and daring to reinvent themselves from the ground up. They actively and continuously *create* the person they want to be.

Awareness is Queen

Now back to your demons. The lurking shadows ready to swallow you whole and determined to inflict unspeakable pain on you. What would you do if a three-year-old was is afraid of the monster in the closet? You would turn on the light and show them there is no monster, right? It's only their mind, making up stories, movements, and sounds.

The same applies to your shadow demons. You fed them power over the years by being afraid of them. You let them grow into insurmountable obstacles that keep you from being free, from being all of you. We all carry pain in our hearts. Pain that seems so big that we'd do anything to never feel it again. The logical reaction of any intelligent being is to avoid it completely. We choose pleasure over pain. We're designed to avoid pain to survive. It's biology.

Yet we're in an evolutionary phase. Not all pain is equal. Sometimes pain is no more than an illusion. Not real. A trick of the demon that rules over the kingdom of the ego. By listening to its toxic advice and avoiding your pain, you also avoid your full potential. That's just what the demon wants because, in the light of your potential, all shadows dissolve and cease to exist.

The key to amplifying your light lies in fully embracing your darkness.

If you're willing to travel into your darkness, you will find that the darkness is an illusion. What you find in your darkness, is your brightest light. The darkness can never extinguish your light. The essence of who you are, the bright light, is available to you if you have the courage to push through the darkness, the pain, the fear to arrive at the core of who you are. That's when you know the truth of your being.

> *"One does not become enlightened by imagining figures of light, but by making the darkness conscious."*
> *– Carl Jung*

The only way out of the games of the ego mind is to shine the light of awareness. Once we become aware of our hidden disempowering beliefs we have a choice. The choice to keep fueling disempowerment or to let go of what no longer serves us. Every disempowering belief is like a layer that distorts our soul's essence. It gets harder to see the light, feel your divinity, and reconnect to your full creator powers.

The layers push you to behave like a robot programmed to do certain things and respond in a certain way. Once you become aware of the programs, you have a choice. You have a free will on this planet. You *always* have a choice. You can choose to let the ego run its programs on you or you can choose to shine the light of awareness. You can choose to buy into the fear that the ego inflicts on you or you can choose to let your essence of love and light rule.

Shine the light of awareness on your disempowering beliefs and choose to substitute them with empowering beliefs. This way you will choose love over fear and your path to purpose becomes clear.

You're light already. There's nothing you need to do to be the light. It's your essence. To understand your truth and fully act from your full potential, you need to become aware of your darkness. Once you are aware that you are slipping into darkness, feeling separate from your Divine essence, you can consciously refocus on your light and your connection to source. Stepping into your full creator powers is not a quest for perfection. It is a journey of consciousness. There is nothing wrong with you that needs fixing. The parts of you that no longer fit your light will be exposed and healed along the way. You are already perfect. Your demons are only the way showers to your most sparkling light.

The ego speaks first and loudest. The heart's voice is gentle, soft, and an intuitive knowing. When was the last time you consciously listened to the guidance of your heart?

The second characteristic of people living their purpose is awareness. Self-awareness comes from observing your thoughts and actions mindfully. When you're mindful of what you do and why you do it, you can take a bird's-eye perspective and see your ego in action from above. You are not your past. You are so much more. You decide who you want to be from now on. By being aware of your motives, desires, and triggers, you can redirect your destiny and create an upgraded version of yourself.

Plug into Power

How would it be if you felt guided and supported every single day by a higher power? Just imagine that you're given unexpected opportunities, ideas, and even people that support your path. Imagine that facing your shadow demons was less of a fight, but rather a surrender into all you can be. Imagine, that living your purpose felt like a warm cloak of healing and not like gearing up to go to war. Imagine having a bigger vision that felt like plugging into a power source that recharges you with motivation and fierce stamina to keep moving? A power so potent that it always comes halfway once you decide to manifest a heartfelt desire?

Plugging into source power basically means attuning yourself to the flow and essence of life. You stop resisting the greatness, abundance, and love your soul and a higher power have in store for you. Instead you begin to see *your* place in the whole of creation. Attuning your mind, body, and spirit to Source, God, the Universe, Spirit (whichever term resonates with you most) lets you access knowledge and powers greater than you can see as a human. You *are* a soul having a human experience, not the other way round. When you attune to your spiritual self you'll find that your energy increases and you feel much more connected to the world around you.

I was once walking through the underground at Alexanderplatz in Berlin at 6:30 pm. If you don't know, first of all, it's the primary intersection of undergrounds in the city — so imagine a huge underground network lined with sterile but colorful tiles, multiple levels of train stops, and people rushing from one subway to the next. I mean, even pigeons hang out down there. So, my point is, it's most likely the busiest and most stressful place in Berlin with everyone commuting and bumping into each other. Especially at rush hour. Usually I'd throw my energetic protection cloak on and get out of there as fast as I could. But that one day, something happened that I'll never forget.

I was getting ready to draw my aura in as I entered the busy levels. To explain, an aura is the energy field around our bodies. Mine has expanded tremendously through my spiritual practice, and if I don't pull it to the outline of my body, lots of people are walking through it. Depending on the person, this can feel very unpleasant. But having hundreds of people walk through your aura or stand in it can stain your aura with pieces from others. Of course you can clear them out again, but it's much more pleasant to just not take them on in the first place. The higher your vibration rises, the more sensitive you will become toward energies.

Back to the story, people were rushing past me, countless stairs, entries, and exits being trafficked by a colorful blend of people. And there I was, preparing to protect me. But what happened absolutely blew my mind: an overwhelming feeling of being *one* with everyone around me washed over me!

My consciousness seemed to expand and the experience was no longer dreadful or painful. I actually felt deep peace, love, and connection with *all that is* in that moment. *We were all ONE.* I didn't have to protect myself. The feeling was so overwhelmingly beautiful that I only made it up one more flight of stairs before I pulled out of the stream of people onto the side to just breathe, enjoy, and feel this experience with every cell of my body. To me it was a *huge* gift. It felt as if I was knighted by a higher power, deemed worthy enough for a profound spiritual experience like this in the place I least expected it. A glimpse of what life could feel like,, when we've reached a point of consciousness that transcends our physical reality. I placed my palms together and silently said, "Thank you" for the confirmation that all the work I've been doing on myself was paying off. I knew I was on the right path to self-realization.

I see this and many other mind-blowing experiences I've had as gifts sprinkled along the path of self-actualization to confirm my course and motivate me to keep going. I think we all have our unique experiences, goals, and dreams. My goal has always been to become the most powerful, wise, and spiritually gifted version of myself. My soul has been loyally guiding me to awaken to who I really am, what I can do, and how I can best contribute to the world with these gifts.

I know, when you are reading this, *your* soul is guiding you as well. Very likely you've reached a point in your life where the superficial answers to life no longer satisfy you.

Your soul is guiding you to resume your rightful place and step up into the most powerful version you can be in this life.

This looks different for each one of us. One isn't better than the other. We have all chosen our purpose for this life. And once you realign with your soul's true path, *everything* will flow toward an increase of your life for yourself and others. This is why attuning to source power is so important. It plugs you into a source of truth, energy, guidance, and wisdom that provides you with all you need to reach your potential and purpose. Not only will you experience increased energy, rapid manifestations of your thoughts and desires, heightened feelings of love and connection, and permanent guidance, but you will also learn to use your spiritual senses again. Your superpowers.

The third characteristic of people living their purpose is spiritual attunement. They cultivate a spiritual connection of meditation, prayer, energy work, or similar to create a relationship with the Supreme. In the strength and clarity of this relationship lies the power to persistence and purpose on your life path. People who live on purpose are humbled by the guidance and support they receive, and they know they are a tool on this planet. The Supreme works through, and with them, at all times. Cultivating and keeping up this relationship is a priority to them.

Give a Damn

Why do you want to find your purpose? What will change once you are living and standing in your truth and power? All my clients have one thing in common: they feel like they can contribute to the lives of others with their gifts.

We all do this in our unique way. Nobody has the same purpose on this earth. Nature doesn't create wasteful abundance. It creates colorful, beautiful, endless abundance that has purpose and joins each other in a joyful dance of mutual support.

In his book, *The Science of Getting Rich*, Wallace Wattles writes, "When things reach you, they will be in the hands of other men, who will ask an equivalent for them. You can only get what is yours by giving the other man what is his."

Living your purpose means contributing to the world in a way that who you're serving will experience an increase in life. But it also means that your experience of life will increase as well. Often contribution has a connotation of over-giving and self-sacrifice. If you've been attentively reading this book, by now you know that this is *NOT* the will of the Supreme. Your Source seeks for greater expression through its individual creations. You are its creation (you're part of the Supreme) and it seeks to express itself more through you and through everyone else. It is the only way to make for more life. You are its channel. Your purpose will always benefit all of life, you and everyone else who gets in contact with it.

What I know for sure? The question, "How can I add more value for my customers?" will always pay back in gold. Deliver more use value than you receive in monetary value. Someone who does purposeful business like this will never be out of a job. A client is not a faceless number on an email list. Really *care* about them. Infuse a bit of your heart into all you create. I'm putting a bit of my heart into every word I write in this book, for instance.

Intention is always felt, even if it's on a subtle energetic level. It transports through time and space.

Let service be your guiding star and don't worry about not having enough. The Universe will always provide to you in abundance when you are on a path of purpose increasing all of life. It must do so to keep increasing its own expression through you.

The fourth characteristic of people living their purpose is contribution. They focus on increasing life for everyone they get in touch with. They ask how they can serve in their biggest and best way. They put themselves in their customers' shoes so they can add tremendous value to their lives. But, they also know it's not selfish to receive back. They see themselves as part of all of life and rejoice in living more fully, freely, and abundantly. They know they need to *have* more, so that they can *use* it to *do* more, *be* more, and *serve* the world more.

Rrrring. Your Soul is Calling

I'll further walk you through the possible challenges along your path so that you can navigate them skillfully. My goal in the last paragraphs was to outline what type of person succeeds at living a purposeful life. Purpose sometimes seems like this intangible "thing" that either you are lucky enough to find or know from early on in your life, or you'll never get it. It's not true. Everyone who is looking for purpose, has a purpose. Including you. Otherwise you wouldn't feel compelled to find it.

Not everyone listens to this calling. And that's okay, too. At every point in time, you can choose differently. With your life came a unique gift: free will choices. So few cultivate the habits and character traits needed to live their full potential. So few persist through the challenges. But those who do are blessed to live an extraordinary life.

I'm not going to sugarcoat it — living your full truth and purpose will challenge you. It's your spiritual calling to self-actualize, to realize who you really are. The fun part is, this path is *your* unique path. While there are markers, motivation, and support along the way, *you* have to walk it to see it. This is where the dreamers are separated from the achievers. Dreamers contemplate a future and build castles in the sky, but never take the necessary actions to manifest their dreams into reality. They dream of what could be, they feel a pull toward it, but they fail to follow through. The achievers (and spiritual warriors) on the other hand do not shy away from adversity, risks, challenges, and uncomfortable experiences.

Don't let this stop your enthusiasm. It's just a fact, that if you were already all that you could be, you'd *already* be living your purpose right now. Right? We need to be realistic. I'm sure you are already above the common crowd in your vision, achievements, and actions, but the thing is, there is still more untapped potential within you. You are just so infinitely more gifted than others who have lower standards of purpose, truth, and power for their life. Deep down you *know* this.

Growing into your full power means letting go of the "half" power that you've achieved until now. And this will challenge you to question yourself, your mindset, your actions, and look at some painful experiences from your past so you can rise above them. It's going to be an extremely empowering and healing growth process. You will never want to go back. I can guarantee you that.

So, close your eyes for one moment. Place your left hand on your heart. Take a deep breath. What does your soul long to do? Follow a path of purpose and elevate into a life of greatness? Or does it long to continue going as is? Notice any feelings, visions, and sensations in your body. Which camp do you belong to?

Are you in the purpose camp? Then let's keep moving...

"Sometimes you have to let everything go — purge yourself.
If you are unhappy with anything — whatever is bringing
you down — get rid of it. Because you will find that when
you are free, your true creativity, your true self, comes out."
– Tina Turner

Puzzles in the Rabbit Hole

Do you ever feel like a unicorn in a herd of horses? I know I did, my whole life. I always felt that, for some incomprehensible reason, I didn't fit in. I seemed to be seeing a different world than the people around me. More intense. More clearly. More raw. No sugarcoating. I'd see through the superficial stories that people were telling themselves, straight to the core of the truth. It was strange for me, because what was so crystal clear, so obvious to me, seemed to be a special gift in other people's eyes.

People around me were enjoying things that had no appeal to me. The "real" world felt gray and harsh to me. I was much of a loner. I wasn't unpopular, I just really enjoyed spending time by myself. I listened to music, dreamed up tales of adventures, grand love stories, and mysterious places. I always longed to be somewhere else, in faraway countries or even galaxies. Earth just didn't feel so much like home to my soul. I was dreaming of superpowers, reading people's minds, sending light from my palms to heal others. I was reading spiritual texts and books about clairvoyance long before I was allowed to drive a car.

My soul had been whispering to me through my imagination, intuition, visions, dreams, desires and heartfelt longings. I didn't always know how to listen and often brushed my intuition aside. I learned to trust my intellect and make logical decisions. The older I got, the more I left my true self at the door and tried to be what others expected of me.

I lost myself. To be honest, I didn't think I had ever truly known myself.

"Care about what other people think
and you will always be their prisoner."
– Lao Tzu

Luckily my soul didn't give up. I could throw layer over layer of conditioning, false beliefs, and fears onto it, but it was still pulsing patiently for me to be ready. Waiting for the right timing, when I would be ready to accept the essence of who I am, the gifts that my soul longed to bring forth and share with the world.

Ultimately, it was waiting for me to *finally* realize that I was stuck on a hamster wheel and although I was going at full speed, I was going nowhere. Probably it was smirking mischievously underneath all these layers at my useless efforts to fit in and giggling with child-like joy when I finally lifted the veil to find it.

It wasn't until I decided to let go of what society wanted me to be that I could become what my soul had planned for me. I was craving the raw truth of life. The magic. The mystery. The higher wisdom of the Buddhas, Jesuses, and Yogis. I was longing for magic with every cell of my being. The successful life I had created was nothing but a shattered illusion that had promised salvation, peace, freedom, and love. It left me hungover with smudged makeup.

Thirty years of trying to fit in and I gave up. I was finally ready to attune to my soul essence. I made meditation and spiritual encounters a daily routine. People couldn't teach me the type of knowledge I was looking for. I figured I'd go straight to the source, literally. I treated my spiritual friends just like my human friends. I'd make appointments to channel messages, guidance, and insights from them. I'd invite them into my mediations to show me visions and help me find my purpose in life so that I could serve a higher goal. You could say I was damn serious about it. I was determined to get rid of every ounce of smallness and mediocrity. I got cracking to release old mindset, conditioning, past life karma, limiting beliefs, and bad habits. It wasn't easy, but every step of the way, I felt more freedom, clarity, and in tune with my truth.

There is no one path to finding purpose. But what I know for sure, is that your purpose will clearly reveal itself once you attune to the essence of who you are. Your gift and purpose is stored within you like a crystalline diamond hovering in your heart center. It radiates from you in everything you are and everything you do. You don't find it, you realize it. You are already one.

By attuning myself to the infinite intelligence of the Universe, I accessed the wisdom stored in it from lifetimes and other dimensions. The pain of seeing things differently that I felt in my childhood revealed itself as my biggest gift. The gift that I can see your essence, your full potential. I also see what's keeping you from accessing this potential, and I can heal it as a channel for source energy.

Not exactly a job description you study for in school.

I took such a big detour to realize my purpose. But once I got it, it all made sense! My biggest gift was to transform my clients. I rapidly changed the way they experienced themselves and their lives. I guided them into their purpose and higher potential. I helped them understand the mysteries of life and begin their own journey of self-actualization. That's why you're reading this book right now. As my service to your purpose. Somehow it found its way to you. You're supported. Smile.

Your purpose is not necessarily one big gift. The *one* thing that you're good at. I think that's where many of us stumble. We access our biggest expression by using all of our gifts, big and small. So, your ambition, vision, stamina, humor, hobbies, etc. all contribute to your unique expression of purpose. It's a bit like a puzzle that you put together. And sometimes you have to try to see whether the pieces fit. And then some of us (ahem, yours truly) try to make pieces fit that simply don't belong together. Instead of creating beauty, they create a big mess of dislocated parts that don't make a harmonious whole. It just looks pathetic, really...

I mean, who would've known that the path to finding and understanding my purpose was to put as many dislocated puzzle pieces together until the pain of living in that puzzle was unbearable.

There was no way of sugarcoating it anymore. I wasn't happy in my job. I wasn't happy with myself. Life didn't work for me. I had to pull the emergency brake. Choose radical honesty over self-illusion. Purge myself from everything and everyone that wasn't contributing to my happiness. I knew I wanted purpose, connection, to help others, and live a good life along the way. I had no idea *how*, but that wouldn't stop me. The pain of continuing down the rabbit hole was too big, I had to get out of there...

CHAPTER 2

BURN BRIDGES, BURN!

"Yesterday I was clever, so I wanted to change the world.
Today I am wise, so I am changing myself."
– Rumi

Big Egos

As I looked up from the white table, I remembered that one simple thought was all it took to turn my life upside down. All it took to put me in this sterile room, closed off in a meeting with the Head of HR. Emotions were welling up, as we discussed the terms of my leave from the company. I had poured my heart and soul into building the department from scratch, early mornings, late nights, canceled private appointments. I lived and breathed that job. I soaked it up into my every pore; I made it who I am.

Now, all I can think of was the foul taste of deceit and disgrace that accompanied the betrayal. I sign the papers and hurry past stylishly clothed employees, barely making it to the nearby bathroom. I need a moment alone. A moment to digest that my life, as I know it, is over. It'll never be the same again. Riddled with fear, all I can concentrate on right now, is to breathe. Just one breath after the other. As if it was the latest en vogue mantra from the Middle East, I keep telling myself I'll be fine. Yet I could feel the ground shaking below my feet.

Not even a year ago, I felt as if I was burning out. I loved my job as Head of Onsite Innovations. I was working for an online and mobile fashion e-commerce company. In many ways unprecedented, one of the few start-up companies that became a huge success. We had grown to 5,000 employees in the last three years and had expanded into multiple new offers and markets. Competitors in our industry kept a watchful eye on us and knew it was safe to copy what we were putting out. I was calling the shots. Everything that the user gets to see or interact with had to go through my approval. My team and I created new and improved features, designs, and apps every single day. I loved it and I loved seeing the team and company thrive. For the past years, we could test and implement in high speed with little bureaucracy. It was us against the world. We'd show them that we'll be successful.

I was the warrior princess: I got up at the crack of dawn to exercise to David Kirsch's New York Body Plan, 8 am I was the first in the office to catch up on emails, then meetings all day, and after 6 pm, quick check-ins with my team members, then, more emails. More often than not, I was the last to leave. Vacation wasn't for me. I didn't need time off from the thrill of being Mrs. Big Shot, well, at least not until I started running low on energy. I started feeling tired and wasn't able to regenerate fast enough to keep up the superwoman pace I set for myself. I wasn't functioning at the level I was used to anymore. I stopped going out on weekends so I could restore my strength and give 150 percent again at work on Monday.

After some time, the company atmosphere started changing, tough. Consultants were hired into key positions. Us against the world turned into one department against the other. Everyone started trying to keep their sheep safe and make progress that they could show their bosses. Since every change went through my team, we were the ones put at the stake from all sides. For a long time, I didn't mind. I was a determined, young, confident women with a cute, short haircut and a direct attitude. I think I heard them refer to me as "intimidating" more than once. It was obvious I meant business. I had little patience or time for sweet talk or building "positive" relationships with other department heads who were mostly men. To me that translated to superficial talk with the goal only to manipulate me into doing what others wanted me to do for them. In truth, I was mainly frustrated that my job's atmosphere was shifting so rapidly from a fun, innovative workplace where I made real impact, to a company with long lines of approval, slow processes, and big egos.

I've always been a spiritual seeker. I meditated every day, read self-help books in my spare time, and attended spiritual growth seminars during vacation. I had an on-off relationship with yoga, but I remembered that it was rejuvenating for my body and mind. When I hit that point close to burnout, nothing seemed to help me regain my strength. So, I figured it was time for a long overdue vacation. I had four full weeks of unused vacation days. Check!

Hanging out by the beach wouldn't actively restore me, I knew that much. I'd come back just as tired as I'd left. I needed something that would fill me up from the inside. As I was looking through options, I was guided to a Yoga Teacher Training starting just weeks from now, far away from everything up in the Himalayan Mountains. I was late for my application and I had little previous yoga knowledge to show, but everything kept falling into place. I got the four weeks off (unheard of until then), my application was granted, the timing was perfect, and the prospect of feeding my soul excited me.

"Silence is the language of God,
all else is poor translation."
— Rumi

Glimpse of Essence

A glimpse of eternity was all it took to change me forever. My legs were still numb from sitting cross-legged on the meditation pillow as I slowly opened my eyes. I will never forget the moment I looked up over to the crystal clear river, carving its way through the high peaks of the Himalayas. It seemed to be the same sight as thirty minutes before, yet everything was different. Little did I know, I had just opened Pandora's box. In a good way, nothing would ever be (or feel) the same again. The answer to my unspoken prayer was revealed.

Breathe in slowly, breathe out slowly. Hold your focus on your third eye. Straight back, don't crouch. Let the thoughts pass by.

Repeat your mantra. Gosh, monkey mind is going crazy again today. My knees hurt and my legs are numb. I wonder if this is so hard for everyone else in the room? I sneak a peek at the other students in the room: all concentrated, sitting upright in silent meditation. Everyone else seems to be in Divine ecstasy. I'm just wondering why the thirty minutes felt so long today. It's not a relief to see the others, so let's just keep at it and go back into meditation practice. Breath. Mantra. Focus.

Moments later, I'm surprised as everything around me turns silent. I'm being pulled up, out of my body. All sounds are gone and I find myself in the most absorbing and peaceful silence. Pure bliss. Pure being. That's when Spirit infused me with an idea that would change me forever. A profound knowing came over me...

I created my life back home.

I created my life. I can create *differently*.

...if I choose to.

In this moment, one with my true essence, I felt my soul speaking to me. I was given a vision of how people all over the world lead different lives. No one's life is the same as another person's life. Similar in goals, desires, or ambitions, but never the same. It was a colorful picture of people busily living their lives, striving, thriving, and dreaming. Everyone is creating their own life. I saw cultures, families, spirituality, desires, and dreams as influences. Every person was just so unique that the life they created always looked different. It wasn't until later that I understood why that was so important.

I knew right then and there that I had to take responsibility. For everything. Not just the good, but also the bad in my life. The reality with all its facets was a creation of my unique being. I created a life that was now making me sick, tired, depleted, and unhappy. My soul was dying and it reached out to tell me: make a change and create a better life.

All I knew at that time was that I wanted to help others. I wanted to know that I touched someone else's life and made it better. I envisioned that once I died, people would remember me and think of how I increased, healed, and positively impacted their lives. My existence had made a difference for others. Having a job was no longer good enough, I wanted *purpose*. I wanted to help, contribute, and make a living doing *that*.

> *"Everything in the Universe is within you.*
> *Ask all from yourself."*
> *– Rumi*

Testing Me

I really wasn't sure how to manifest the dream my soul had shown me that day. I had taken four stages of life coach training, psychic practices, and energy healings in my free time over the past years. I knew this was part of my essence, something I'm naturally good at. So, I had been asking my angels and the Universe to give me guidance on the next best steps for me to transition into a new purposeful career. Although on some level I felt so ready to leave the old life behind, I was also scared. I had built a really nice life for myself. Great salary, status in society, lots of comfort. My spiritual guidance kept telling me that it wasn't yet time to make a move. So I stayed put. My friends know that patience was not my strength back then. I had more of a "I'll force it into happening" type of mentality. But I was pursuing a new path and I was listening to a higher power. My faith in the Supreme grew with every soothing message I received. I kept focusing on getting ready to jump, once my essence would tell me to.

I practiced my psychic senses, practiced my energy healing skills, and did anything to reconnect to my soul's essence. In the Himalayas, I had received a "fix" of connectedness to the Universe, a deep peace, and I was craving more. I was hungry for it.

After a few months, nothing really seemed to happen on the surface. Probably the Universe was working in the background as it always does. Circumstances at work got more frustrating and an office relocation split our department in two, isolating my team and me in a new location. I was ready to make a move on my dreams and wanted to apply for a job in New York City. I had the integrity to let my boss know I was toying with the idea of progressing to the next job.

The next thing I knew, I found myself in the closed-off meeting room discussing the terms of my leave. No backup. No new job. My boss had just told me the day before that "we" were leaving. I felt betrayed in my trust to share my plans. I felt disappointed in the company that I had poured my heart and soul into. I never fully understood what workings were at play that orchestrated my leave, but one thing I knew for sure…

It was happening *for* me.

It was not happening *to* me.

I had caused the Universe to create a situation at the perfect time for me to step into my fuller potential. È voilà! There it was!

The day I sent the goodbye email to all my business partners, I received a phone call. I was offered an even better job at a luxury fashion company. In retrospect I have to smile because I know exactly what the Universe was doing. It was giving me a chance to bail out of my intention to create a new life being on purpose. It gave me a parachute. Double the pay, a Director title, influence on the management board, and an interesting job description was an upgrade all around! In my gut, I knew it wasn't right for me. But I felt compelled to take it. This was the type of job I was working toward all my life. I mean, all the years spent in school, college, and long work hours, working my way up the corporate ladder. It seemed like the grand prize!

After a month, I realized I had gone too far exploiting my soul. The corporate world had no appeal to me anymore. I couldn't even muster up enough ambition to start building the new department. I remember how my shoulder started hurting constantly and that the job felt like a burden to me. I took the parachute the Universe handed me and now I couldn't wait to get down to the ground fast enough. I slit open my metaphorical Swiss knife and cut the cords on the parachute: I quit after two months to pursue my dream life of helping people. How? I still had no idea. I was free falling from status, six-figure income, titles, and bonuses. The ground was approaching at deadly speed. Who knows if I had done it, had I known that things were about to get really challenging from there.

"Forget safety.
Live where you fear to live.
Destroy your reputation.
Be notorious."
– Rumi

Burn Bridges Burn

In the next year I started exploring different ideas. I played around to get funding for a coaching and meditation app, I had several business ideas, all of which didn't put me at the forefront. It was a long inner journey for me to accept that my business would revolve around me as a person and that I would have to be visible in my essence.

What nagged at me was the fact that my rekindled spirituality felt like the only real thing in my life, yet I was scared to own it. I'm a down-to-earth person and even though I experienced it firsthand and my heart knew the truth, I was afraid people would label me as crazy. It did sound a bit crazy, even to me, that I talked to angels and offered energy healings using my psychic senses. I was torn between my old identity of the business woman and my true essence of a spiritual teacher. Many told me that I was committing "corporate suicide." I didn't care. To me, it felt like the ground was being pulled from under my feet and I was leaping. I didn't see land anytime soon, so I was still free falling. On the way down, I was wondering whether I just committed real-life suicide or whether a net would catch me at some point. This was it. Bridges burned.

What followed was far from gracious. You hear the stories of how someone quit their job and they made a bazillion dollars in the first year of their business? Yeah, that wasn't me.

After the first year of exploring ideas that weren't aligned with my essence, I finally accepted that I was a crazy psychic business woman who had gifts to share with the world. I started my coaching business and loved every one of my clients. It was exhilarating to see their rapid transformations and thirst for growth. Although I was finally making some money, my ambitions were much higher and I felt like a failure. The pressure I put on myself to "get it right" was insurmountable. I had been spending my savings for two years now with no bulletproof recipe to make big bucks like so many others online.

I crumbled under my own expectations. I've always been a perfectionist and I knew it would come around to bite me someday. But the sense of failure wasn't enough. I was always resourceful, so I found a "great" way to impose endless physical and psychological pain on me: an eating disorder. Bulimia had been with me ever since I entered the workforce.

Remember how I never felt like I fit in? Well, everything in life comes with a price and I had to pay mine for fitting into a world that was never meant for me. When I was participating in the grown-up world, bulimia was my refuge, my rescue to gobble it all down and sedate myself to not feel the emptiness within me.

Looking back, I understand its message: "Girl, you're not on track, you're detouring from your soul's path. Turn around!" I just didn't understand it. Before, I could "only" binge and purge once a day because I was at work. But being able to manage my own time, things got out of hand. Bulimia became my safe place when I felt overwhelmed. And everything felt overwhelming and scary. I was still free falling and bulimia was my only companion on the way down. Its presence was the ultimate confirmation that something was inherently wrong with me. Why can't I just eat like normal people?! It was a daily reminder how weak and pathetic I was.

Determined to figure this online business thing out, I kept investing more money in courses and mentors, while killing myself softly behind the scenes. On the surface, I was always onto the next project and getting things done. I am ambitious. I thought by now I'd be making six figures in my own business. Yet, no huge successes came rolling around. Nothing. Nada.

I still remember the day I gave up. I was walking home from the grocery store with a bag full of food I was ready to binge on. I said to the Supreme, "I'm done. This is too hard. I give up. If you don't want me helping people like this, then so be it. The pain is too big and I'm done struggling." I got ready to look for jobs, but instead I got flashes of inspiration and a vision. I started channeling my first meditations as a Self-Love Course. It was amazing to feel Spirit speak through me, to see visions of angels and fairies. The whole experience of creating this course was an initiation into more power. Okay, let's face it, at that moment — *I* was the one who *really* needed that course. I created it for me, just as much as I did for everyone else out there. I got phenomenal reviews from my clients and was back, hooked to serve. Spirit sure knows how to spark our motivation.

I had been trying to get rid of bulimia for ten years. No success. I had tried to find my authentic business model that would fulfill my purpose. No success.

But there was one skill that played into my cards. I was stubborn and hardheaded. I wasn't going to give up. I may adjust and stay flexible. But when I want something, I'm like a Pitbull clenching its teeth into flesh. I felt like a vampire licking blood for the first time and it got me hooked. I wanted more.

Now is the point in the story where I tell you I let go of bulimia and made a million bucks in a month. Hmm, no. Sorry to disappoint.

It took me a few more months to understand that nothing was wrong with me for having bulimia and that my brain was just sending impulses of survival to my body. How fitting to my situation, don't you think? I did let go of the inner struggle of food that had disconnected me from the world and caused more pain than I'd ever wish on anybody. I put the war with my body to rest and started loving myself wholeheartedly.

When it came to my purpose, I could finally own one of my biggest truths: I'm not a business woman, per se. I'm a teacher, a messenger, a spiritual mentor, and catalyst. My dream has always been to be an author and to help people transform. The only way I was able to get here was to let go of all the expectations I laid on myself in terms of success, time frames, image, and money. As long as I tried to control how I would serve, I wasn't aligned with the way my soul craved to serve. Only as I was able to surrender the *how*, let go of *how* I wanted success to unfold, I was able to realign with my essence and full authentic truth. That's when my psychic sense started skyrocketing in the most beautiful ways and when my purpose started supporting me. Not the other way around. No more pushing and forcing.

Live Your Truth

This is what my work is about. Helping my clients shed the weight of their burdens and heal on a holistic level, let go of disempowering mindset and expectations of society, reconnect to their essence for intuitive guidance and detect their biggest gifts so that they can lead a life on soulful purpose. When they accept their truth, their essence, they are able to *surrender* into their power. You *are* powerful; it's not something you have to force into being.

Sam, for instance, found me as he stared at the results Google spit out for him. He had just lost his corporate job, his soul mate, and had no idea what to do next. One of the first results that popped up was my video, "Why it's a good sign your life is falling apart." Later he would tell me that he was wondering what type of crazy lady I must be for thinking that a life falling apart is a *good* thing! The video resonated with him and he soon became a private client of mine. He was carrying so much pain, despair, and disempowering energetic weight, it was a testament to his strength that he was still standing. He was discouraged and disappointed with how life had treated him. He didn't think he could get up one more time, just to be beat down again. His hope, energy, and zest for life felt gone.

Through our work we were able to release past-life beliefs, agreements and energy imprints so that he could finally feel a shift in his energy levels. We cleared out family cords and relationships that were harmful and constantly recreated a vicious cycle that kept him stuck in pain and powerless. He started meditating and clearing his chakras regularly. He put the spiritual tools that I'll be sharing with you here into practice. He was finally reattuning to his soul essence and started receiving spiritually guided proof of his gifts, talents, and purpose.

After a few weeks of working together, he told me that he felt like a completely different person! Only a short time had passed, but he was on a completely different and more powerful path. Instead of being stuck in a rut of self-sabotage, victimhood, and flat-out pain, he was now looking at a career as a speaker and teacher to serve with his story. On top of that, he believed that there was another perfect woman out there for him.

Many of my clients transform their lives rapidly and entirely. One key insight that I got from my really painful path, is that realigning with your *truth*, with who you *really* are, doesn't have to be hard. The more radically you surrender to your truth, the easier, faster, and smoother your transformation into joy and purpose will be.

Are you ready to surrender? Yes? Great.

Now, surrender harder.

(You'll understand soon.)

"Only surrender to your truth,
never to challenges along your path."
— Yours truly

CHAPTER 3

YOUR PURPOSE MANIFESTO

"If one advances confidently in the direction of his dreams,
and endeavors to live the life which he has imagined, he will
meet with a success unexpected in common hours."
– Henry David Thoreau

The Seed of Purpose

Take a walk with me through a meadow of rich flowers. The summer sun is sitting high in the sky, birds are chirping, bees are flying from blossom to blossom. The meadow is surrounded by trees, as if to protect its delicate beauty. On the horizon you notice high, peaceful mountains, their tips covered in snow. It's a graceful, Divine place. You inhale with a deep breath and smell the diverse scents of summer from the abundant nature around you. You enjoy the serenity of the moment and start to gently stroll through the high grass and flowers. Your hands are reaching out and you let your fingertips softly brush up against the high grass. As you are setting down one foot after the other, your mind wanders to contemplate the essence of the flowers.

You notice that not one is the same as another, even those that are the same kind. Each one has grown differently or has a slightly different shade of color or even a different count of flower buds. The variety of flowers strikes you as an infinite abundance. The meadow lighting up in countless shades of colors is truly a gift. Walking among the flowers, you also notice something else. Something you never quite thought of before, but now in the peacefulness of the moment, standing so consciously among the beautiful flowers, it becomes clear to you.

Each flower is unique, yes, but each flower is also blossoming to its full capacity. None of the flowers are holding back their beauty. They are in different stages, of course; some are only flower buds and others are in full bloom. Yet every flower shares its full expression openly, willingly, and fully. They are not competing with each other for which is the most dazzling of them all. They grow into their full bloom without hesitation and without haste. They share their full expression with everyone who seeks to rejoice in it. And if someone doesn't, they don't care; they still grow into all they can be. Strolling further along, you let this idea simmer down into your subconscious and you realize…

You are a creation of unique beauty from the one essence of life, just like the flowers. You have your own timing and pace to grow into full bloom. Whether others rejoice in your beauty or not is none of your concern. You know that life wants to pulse through you to its fullest capacity, and you are willing to let the essence of life find its fullest expression in you. Everything else would mean holding back the flow of life and trying to stay as a flower bud, while you are meant to be in full bloom.

Maybe hesitating slightly, you realize your heart has been waiting for this very moment all along. The moment in which you realize that there is so much *more potential* within you that is still untapped, unexplored territory. The moment in which you decide to realign yourself with all you can be and reclaim your power as a Divine creator on a mission. The insight alone is not enough though. The seed is planted, but it needs water to grow.

You'll need to dedicate yourself to the journey of reconnecting to your soul's essence. Then your full purpose, potential, happiness, and fulfillment are guaranteed.

Warrior Essence

Most of us go through life making the best of our circumstances. We advance, succeed, and achieve, yes. But still we move within the lines that family and society sets for us. We dim down our heart's fire to adhere to responsibilities laid on us and expectations imposed on our spirit. It starts when we're only kids. Most of us have grown up being taught that we need to follow a certain path — school, college, job, partner, house, kids. That's the good life. We're told that's the recipe for happiness. And it works for all of us.

But many of the generations who are now in their twenties, thirties, and forties realize it's not the good life. Not for them. While this was a great way of life for our parents who thrived into wealth after our grandparents set the foundation of survival, for many of us, this is not happiness or fulfillment.

Our generation is unique because the planet is ascending into a higher frequency of love and light. Special kids have been born in our generation: Indigo children. Not all of us are Indigos or on a mission to self-actualize. That's why many still feel happy, living a safe and comfortable lifestyle based on old paradigms. They don't feel like there is a higher purpose or a deep calling from their soul to wake up to who they really are. That's okay. One isn't better than the other, just different.

Indigos are spiritual movers, shakers, and trailblazers. They are the first wave of spiritual lightworkers with important life purposes. Indigos have a fierce warrior spirit because their collective purpose is to tear down all systems that lack integrity. They are highly sensitive, empathic, and psychic. Be aware — Indigos know when they are being lied to. They have the important role of paving the way for humanity to step into a higher vibration of love and light. Indigos can sometimes feel like they don't belong. They often feel like outsiders. They may even feel like they have nothing to contribute to the existing world. They are so aware of the imbalance on earth that they sometimes wonder how they could ever fit in. The thing is, *they (you) aren't meant to fit in*! It is their gift and purpose to clearly see the necessary shifts for humankind. They are not meant to be silenced in the face of adversity, but they are meant to lead into a new era of conscious living. They were born from the 1970s onward, and with their warrior energy they pave the way for the second "specialization" of lightworkers, the Crystal Children.

The Crystal Children are not warriors; they are even tempered and blissful. They exude a sense of peace, love, forgiveness, and they are wise beyond their years. Their eyes mirror the wisdom of their soul. As much as the Indigos have blasted the path free for a revolution, the Crystal Children's task is to *build* the new world based on higher values.

A very new breed of lightworker has appeared on our planet called the Rainbow Children. Doreen Virtue explains on her website that the Rainbow Child is born to Crystal Children who are coming into adulthood now. She says that they are an embodiment of divinity and an example of our full potential. They have already reached their spiritual peak and never lived on our planet before. Crystal Children are fearless, givers, and all about service for others. The terms Indigo, Crystal, and Rainbow Children, by the way, derive from the predominant aura colors of these people.

How do you know whether you're one of them? You already know. Probably while reading, you felt a part within you resonate; maybe you teared up, maybe your heart expanded, or you were thinking "yes." It can also just be a sense of knowing anything goes. Trust your intuitive feelings, no matter how illogical it may seem to you right now.

Ray of Might

You feel you are here for a purpose? You feel you don't fit into society? You look around and wonder why nobody else sees how the system is failing? That's because you are special. You see it because you are meant to fulfill your role as a leader on earth. Your soul chose to lead the way into a new era of existence. You picked up this book now because it's time. You are needed. Your time *on purpose* has come. There is no more time for you to waste in meaningless jobs, pursuing unfulfilling goals.

You've picked up this book because you can sense that a more purposeful life is available to you. I'm here to tell you: Yes, there is. It doesn't even have to be spiritual. Many Indigos are working their trailblazing in nonspiritual ways. Of course, everything contributes to all of life, which is source, so it can never be separated. But in our 3D world, it doesn't seem spiritual. So, don't think you suddenly have to become a "lightworker," whatever that is, right? All you need to do is to follow your soul's calling and discover your essence.

In your essence you will find your truth, your talents, your desires, and a grand vision on how you can create a powerful life for yourself and others. You are meant to be an inspiration, a way shower for others to follow you. Synchronistically, I just watched the movie *Man of Steel* yesterday. Superman's (Kal-El's) father, Jor-El, said something so wise and profound that it blew my mind. I love finding deep truths that resonate with my soul in places where I least expect them. It reminds me of how synchronistic this Universe is and that Spirit is in everything and everyone, always giving us clear guidance. Beautiful.

"You will give the people an ideal to strive towards. They will race behind you, they will stumble, they will fall. But in time, they will join you in the sun [light]. In time, you will help them accomplish wonders."
— Jor-El, Man of Steel

My wish for you is that you understand, with every cell of your being, that you are here for a reason. You were guided to this book for a reason. You are reading these sentences right here, right now, for a reason.

It's *your* time to step into all that you came here to be. You feel it as a desire to be in the flow of life, a desire to thrive, to be free, to stand in your truth, a desire to expand and live a greater life.

In order to get there, you need to realize and acknowledge your true self. The essence of who you really are on a soul level. Your talents, gifts, desires. Your immortal soul carries the wisdom and strength of lifetimes and seeks full expression through your physical self. Now is the time to draw upon your full might.

The path to let go of pain is to surrender to your essence and recognize who you really are: a soul seeking its full purposeful expression in a human body. A warrior ready to clear the path for a new world, with new rules to be built upon.

What would it feel like to accept, integrate, and live your deepest truth? A truth that has been with you through the centuries, dimensions, and lifetimes? What would it be like to rekindle a fire that nourishes and empowers your soul?

Once this light within you is ignited, you'll tap into your full potential and gain the confidence, motivation, and desire to reach it. So, are you ready for a life in tune with the mystery of the cosmos, while all of life is driving you forward and cheering you on?

Come on, Kal-El! Let's get out there and inspire people to do wonders!

"You'll see it when you believe it."
– Dr. Wayne Dyer

Finding Your Essence

By now, you're beginning to grasp that your life purpose is not a destination, per se. There isn't one definite outcome and a straight path to achieve it. We're trained to think that way, sure — study law and you'll be a lawyer. The mystery of life just doesn't work that way. The Universe doesn't work in a linear line. Just us humans think that way because we are so trained to see linearity in our actions. We humans want guarantees and straight lines. We want to control *how things will come to us*. If we just knew exactly what to do and when to do it and we're guaranteed a certain outcome, *then* we'd do it. We treat our lives like a competition and the one with the most awards (shiny objects) wins. But what's the use of being the richest man in the graveyard when you've spent your whole life miserable and out of tune with your essence?

Your purpose may grow as you grow. You evolve and with it your purpose evolves and amplifies. The scream you're hearing from the depths of your soul is a calling for you to reconnect with your true essence, so that you can fill your place on this earth. Your purpose is to explore your full potential from a place of passion and zest for life. Source guides you to ignite the Divine spark within you, that will carry you to the fulfillment, happiness, and abundance that only a life on purpose, in flow with the Universe, can offer.

This journey back to living from your essence will challenge you to grow, overcome fears, and push you to be more of who you really are. It's not always a walk in the park, but nobody (nobody!) is better equipped for this journey than you are. It will be more rewarding than anything you've ever experienced before. Promise.

Your life purpose is not what you do,
it's who you become in the process.

I'll show you how to discover your life purpose by reconnecting with your soul essence because that's where all your wisdom and power is stored. Although we'll need to be really courageous to think and act outside the box, we'll have a lot of fun in the process.

This book is a channel. I'm opening myself up to share with you the information I'm receiving from my guides, angels, celestials, and other light beings. They are here to crack you open to the truth and essence of who you are. The creation of this book has been and continues to be pure magic. The right ideas find me at the right time. Everything falls into place in Divine timing, and all I need to do is show up every day, put my fingers on the keyboard, and write down the words Source puts in my head and heart.

I'm sharing this because I can only teach you what I know to be true. I pass along my truth infused with my soul essence. The steps I'm laying out are one way of finding your purpose and creating a relationship with the mystery of life, but it is not the only way. If for whatever reason this is not for you, then please keep looking for your purpose through another resource. You're ready! I outline the steps of your purpose journey and give you the tools to get clarity, guidance, and transformation. But I can't walk your path for you. I can (and will) cheer you on, but it is your free will how far you will go.

The journey back to your essence will guide you through a series of soulful steps. You will take inventory of your life so that you can know for sure what aspects of it are serving your essence and which ones aren't. I will guide you to explore your soul essence so that you can get a deeper understanding of your true spiritual nature. You have a unique composition of strengths that will serve you on your path of purpose. Many of them you may already be using, some of them you may have forgotten, and some of them may be new to you. Our goal is for you to see yourself in your greatest expression. We don't rush these processes; steady progress is more important than reaching some fictitious end goal.

I'll teach you how to create a relationship with the Supreme so that you feel confident, safe, and guided along your path. This relationship is *the* game changer on your journey. In order to communicate with your essence and draw from its power, you need to relate to it in harmony. You tap back into your power and draw upon source energy to manifest your life deliberately.

One of the most important tools I can give you is how to deal with fears and other mindset blocks that are distorting your connection to your soul essence and purpose. Disempowering beliefs and old conditioning lead you further away from your truth and keep you stuck in old patterns and habits, immobilized to create a better life for yourself. You will learn how to shed the layers of illusion like layers of an onion. With each one shed, you'll reunite more with the truth of your essence. You'll feel clearer and stronger to overcome any obstacles on your path.

None of the steps and tools I share with you will work though, unless you make them work. Like I said, I can't take this journey for you. It is *your* most sacred journey and privilege to be here and to decide *for* it. I will help you understand what inspired action looks and feels like so you can confidently and faithfully take the steps toward living your true purpose.

But before I give you exact tools, exercises, and meditations to reconnect to your soul essence, let me prepare you by outlining the biggest challenges you will face on this journey.

"I'm starting with the man in the mirror;
I'm asking him to make a change;
And no message could've been any clearer,
If you wanna make the world a better place,
take a look at yourself and then make that change."
– Michael Jackson

The Nine Pledges to Purpose

Maybe you're thinking you'll test the waters and see what this whole soul essence and purpose thing is. That's fine. And I think everyone should. In this chapter, I'll address the biggest challenges and tell you how you can overcome them. Everything can be figured out. Even a desire in your heart that you can't yet fully place. That's where we all start. So just know, there is a way to figure out how to live a life that is authentic to you and that has meaning beyond yourself. People have gone before you and their success leaves traces like footprints in the sand. They are not more special, chosen, or worthy than you are. You are here to fulfill *your* purpose. Only you can do it. You are perfectly designed to achieve it. You *can* do it.

Pledge #1
Personal Growth

As much as we humans want change, we're afraid of it. Deliberately and lastingly changing ourselves — gosh, the Oscars of personal development. Now, of course, you *are* already perfect. Nothing is wrong with you or anyone else walking this earth. But, and now listen up, there is always room for becoming a better *version* of yourself. The better version of you is the version where your strengths, talents, and gifts are amplified and you are fiercely living and creating from that place.

You are perfect, because you have unique talents, gifts, and characteristics that make you who you are, but how much of it are you using to its full potential? How often are you held back by limiting beliefs, fears, destructive habits, and past conditioning without even realizing it? I know it's a trick question because basically, you can't know. Just trust me for now; it's often. When you start implementing mindfulness, self-inquiry, and awareness into your days, you soon realize just how few of your decisions are made consciously. Your subconscious has an overpowering impact on you. A whopping 98 percent of your mind belongs to the subconscious and it influences your actions and habits without you consciously noticing.

The other day, I was sitting at a dinner table with a close friend of mine. We were celebrating my birthday at the Soho House in Berlin. It's a very stylish and classy atmosphere overlooking the famous Alexanderplatz in Berlin. A prime spot to see the building that I worked at during my corporate career. We had met just five years earlier in exactly that company. It was bff love at first sight — needless to say, she was a more or less silent observer of my path to more purpose in my life.

That evening she was telling me how much she enjoyed some aspects of her job, but at the same time hated others. She loved the topics she was working on, and at the same time despaired because she had hardly slept in a week. I could see it in her face — she was worn down and depleted, only holding up to deliver her work because of deadlines and stress. After a while she asked me how I was, and how things were going in my business. I told her that I felt relieved and excited because I finally realigned myself with one of my deepest desires: being an author! She looked at me with a gaze of curious astonishment, "I could never do what you do. You're always questioning your motives and work so much on yourself. I could never go through all that." ...words from the woman who hadn't slept in a week. For her, and there is no judgment, it was okay to go through the pain and stress of not sleeping and wearing her body and mind down. But challenging herself to ask uncomfortable questions about fears, motives, desires, dreams, and picking herself up time after time was just not an option for her.

We all have to pick and choose our battles. My path was clearly not the right one for her. She had a different vision of her life and there is nothing wrong or right with it. She just doesn't have the desire and inner calling to contribute to the world in the way I desire to. Same the other way round. She simply has a different path.

I'm telling you this because my friend and I, we're both ambitious, kind, loving, yet fierce female powerhouses. We have a lot in common and care deeply about each other. Yet our souls crave for different experiences in this life. I desire to live my full truth while making a positive impact on others. I desire to grow every single day of my life into more of what I can be. I'm not able to speak for her, but from what she said, that doesn't seem to be part of what she wants in life (maybe yet). She wants to progress and develop, yes. Probably in her career, talents, hobbies, relationships, and other areas. But flush the dirt from her childhood up to the surface to release it? Nope, thank you, pass. Again, that's okay, as long as it's what you feel is *right for you*.

I'm telling you this so that you can decide who *you* are. On a path of purpose, you will have to look at your fears, beliefs, conditioning, and shadows so that you can let them go. You let them go,, so that you're no longer steered by your subconscious and past conditioning that is basically keeping you right where you are. Looping in the same circles. You rise into your fuller potential by empowering your essence through shedding the false mindset patterns. Building on your strengths and letting go of what is not serving you. Go into this journey with open eyes. The process will be liberating, exciting, interesting, and grand, but it will also challenge you to your core. Diamonds are only born under pressure, darling!

Personal Growth Mindset:

- Remind yourself that the inner work will reap huge external and internal benefits.
- The shadow demons (fears) you've been avoiding keep you stuck in a rut, a prisoner in your own life — it's time to break free and shine!
- Stay aware and present with your emotions and reactions. Inquire *why* you're feeling this way so you can uncover old belief systems and exchange them for new, empowering ones.
- Remind yourself why you're growing to stay motivated.
- Radical self-acceptance — everything you feel is valid. It wants and needs to be seen and felt, so that you can release it.

Personal Growth Mastery:

- Download the free interactive workbook: sharonkirstin.com/bookbonus
- Take out your journal: Did you ever work on yourself? Did you let go of a habit that no longer served you? How did you feel after mastering it? Describe it in detail.
- Did you ever get an energy healing, aura cleanse or past-life healing? How did your life change afterward? How did you feel? Be specific.
- Idea #1: Find a community of like-minded people to support you.

- Idea #2: Get a mastermind buddy and support each other to grow faster.
- Idea #3: Hire a coach to help you unleash your full potential.
- Idea #4: Find an energy healer to help you heal past trauma and pain.

It's my purpose to guide as many people as possible into their purpose, truth, and potential. If my work resonates with you, you may like the support I can offer. Just know you're not alone and you have options. Check it out here: www.sharonkirstin.com

Pledge #2
Discomfort

Remember the story I just told you about my friend? She witnessed firsthand how uncomfortable I've been on my path. There was no security blanket that I could grab or land I could climb on. I was swimming in open water with no land in sight. Many times I didn't know whether my strategies, ideas, or creations would even work out the way I wanted them to. Most of the time they didn't. But I chose to keep swimming anyway. I adjusted my course and kept going. Was it comfortable? No. Was it satisfying? Sometimes. Was it necessary? Yes.

If you don't endure the discomfort of doing something new, failing, and still keep on going, you will not be able to get new results in your life. Einstein gave us the brilliant definition of insanity: Doing the same thing over and over while expecting different results.

When you stay in your comfort zone, rarely do big amazing new things happen, or do they? They happen when you take that crazy trip, or when you go to a seminar that it so out of character, or when you get uncomfortable and talk to the cute guy at the bar. *Comfort is the nemesis of progress.* When following your purpose, you really progress into more of you. Step into your soul essence and let every pore of your body radiate this essence out into the world.

I have no idea how the caterpillar feels when it's about to cocoon. What I do know is that in that cocoon, the caterpillar disappears. It's chaos in there. A big fat mess. After a while, the caterpillar is dissolved into an undefinable substance from which the butterfly is created — from scratch. What seems like a very uncomfortable and challenging growth process is actually guided all along. The cells needed to create wings, legs, eyes, and other parts of the butterfly are in the caterpillar's DNA.

Yes, growth pains will occur. Yes, you will have to get uncomfortable more than once. Yes, you will have to endure times of insecure outcomes. Yes, you may feel like a hot mess at times. BUT, if you (the caterpillar) feel called to find your purpose and live a life true to your essence (as the butterfly), then you can rest assured that you already have *all* it takes (it's in your genes) to make that transition. You are made for purpose!

Discomfort Mindset:

- Leave your comfort zone regularly, at least once a week. Know that the uncomfortable feeling will dissipate the more you do it.
- Trust that you have strong wings that will carry you through your transformation and beyond.
- Your journey will challenge you. You'll want to give up at times. Just because it's your purpose doesn't mean you won't have to work for it or grow into it.

Discomfort Mastery:

- When was the last time you did something for the first time? How did it feel? Be specific.
- When was the last time you did something completely out of character? What happened as a result? Did it change you? Explain.
- Idea: Get a coach who's been there and can guide you with grace. (Want me? Learn more here: sharonkirstin.com)

"It's never crowded along the extra mile."
– Dr. Wayne Dyer

Pledge #3

Persistence

If I could only count the times I said to myself: "If this is my purpose, then why (why?!) is this so haaaaard?!" For some reason, people (me included back then) think that creating a life true to them will be a breeze, while a life not honoring their essence is hard. It's slightly different.

Both are challenging — yet the rewards are different.

Living a life that's not true to you, in which you feel trapped, is a source of suffering. Suffering is an intensified form of pain. When you suffer, you believe that you have no power to change your current situation. There is no way out, so you arrange yourself around it. You count the days to the weekend and to the holidays. You design your life around the times you are off from work, or whatever else creates suffering for you, so that you can live those two weeks and fifty-two weekends of the year as you wish. What kind of a life is that?! You spend two-thirds of your life unhappy and try to make it up with the other one-third.

Living your truth and purpose will be challenging, but the major difference is this: fulfillment. At the end of the day, you'll feel like what you did that day mattered to you and someone else. You may work just as hard as before, you choose, but you'll do it with a sense of pride, joy, and meaning. It'll feel different because what you're working for is no longer sucking the life out of you. You're not working for money, but for a meaning. Your work's purpose brings you more to life! It's bringing more life to you and everyone who crosses your path. You will know exactly why you're showing up for, every, single, day.

For this scenario to work, you'll need persistence. Many have a dream to sail the oceans but they rarely make it out of the safe harbor. They console themselves by saying that they tried, but "it wasn't meant to be."

God helps those who help themselves. If your intention is to test the waters and see how it goes, you're not serious about your purpose. Spirit knows. Spirit will only show up as much as you do to support you. If you won't give it your all because you're scared to fail, be ridiculed, or lose time or money, then this adventure may really not be for you. Only you know.

To realize and become all that you can be is the biggest adventure of your life. It's so exciting because it is so unique to you! Nobody else will ever be able to fill your place. Either you do it or nobody ever will. What it takes is passion, motivation, faith, flexibility, and stamina. It takes persistence and flexibility because you will fail more than once to build the life of your dreams. But one thing is clear: you will have to get up one more time than you've been beaten down. Only those who stay down, truly fail in life.

Persistence Mindset:

- Be willing to lose sight of the safe shore to discover a new life.
- Stay flexible in your approach and try different paths to success. It's never a straight line; you will have to test and try what resonates with you.

- Be persistent in pursuing a purposeful life that fulfills you every day. The more you put into finding your success, the faster it'll appear. Spirit supports you.

Persistence Mastery:

- List at least three goals in your life that you've reached because you pursued them with persistence, flexibility, confidence, passion, and/or motivation. Write them down.
- Remind yourself of all the successes you've had until now in your life. Make a list!
- When have you endured adversity, insecure outcomes, or a period of suffering? How did you overcome it? Remember your strength! Be specific.
- Explain to yourself why you're the perfect candidate to design a life you love with passion and purpose. Trust me; you'll be your worst critic, so let's see if you are convinced.
- Idea: I've prepared an exclusive, free workbook for you to help you move through this journey of finding and living your truth: sharonkirstin.com/bookbonus

"We keep ourselves so tied up in regretting the past and fearing the future that we don't have any energy left to figure out who we are and what we want to create right now."
– Gay Hendricks

Pledge #4

Courage

Nelson Mandela once said, "I learned that courage was not the absence of fear, but the triumph over it. The brave man is not he who does not feel afraid, but he who conquers that fear." Words from a man who was incarcerated for forty years and when he came out, he wasn't a broken soul. He was stronger than ever to fight for his cause. He didn't pity himself for being a victim; instead he used the time in jail to prepare for what he was about to accomplish. Mind-blowing.

Fear is a part of us. We can't expect to embark on any new endeavor without fear popping up and saying, "Hey, sweetie, that's not safe. How about we stick to what we know, okay?" Courageous people aren't fearless, they just do it anyway. They don't listen to the bad, one-dimensional advice of fear. Fear is a primal instinct that has the task to keep you alive. It will do *anything* to stop you from walking in front of the car going by, jumping from the bridge, or walking through that dark alley.

Unfortunately, fear doesn't stick to giving advice in life or death situations. It thinks it has valid advice about everything you do. Sometimes it has a good point. Often it doesn't.

When we were designed, we got an ego in our package. Our ego is the part of us that constantly wants to detour us from realizing our divinity. It wants us to stay stuck in the day to day struggle.

Rising above fear will be a daily habit of yours on this path to purpose. Fear will tell you, it's not safe to follow your passion. It will use any and every trick it has up its sleeve to make you stop. The ego doesn't want you to self-actualize. You realizing your essence means *death to the ego*. Once you realize that you are more than a human, that you are, in fact, one with the cosmos, one with all that is, powerful beyond measure, that you are safe and held in the infinite intelligence of the Universe...would you still listen to the nasty voice inside you that belittles you and others? Of course not. The ego knows that.

How are fear and the ego connected? The Ego's most powerful warrior is fear. The Ego is the kingpin on the throne and fear is its muscle-packed executioner, standing to the right of its throne. The ego is the strategist, always coming up with new tricks to make you feel vulnerable, doubtful, and like you're not enough. Fear will go toe to toe with you in the ring and challenge you until only one of you is left standing.

Imagine fear being this pumped up guy that always hang out at the gym and lifts weights in front of the mirror. Fear has a lot of pumped up muscle, but little strength behind it. Do you know where fear gets its strength? From your emotional reaction to the scenarios the ego puts in your head.

Fear feeds off of *your* strength. The more you're afraid of the false predictions of the Ego, the faster fear will beat you. If you face it head-on and say, "Okay, show me what you got!" do you know what will happen? It'll be like a scene from a movie, where a scary looking guy runs toward you from a distance. In the beginning you're scared, you want to run away, hide, do something. The last thing you want is to get into a fist fight with muscle-guy, right? But you hesitate and realize something: the closer he gets, the more you notice that he is short. Really short. Tiny. Finally he approaches you and you have to control yourself not to laugh as he only reaches up to your knees! A lot of muscle, but would you be afraid of a little executioner like that? Probably not.

Fear can only stop you if you let it. If you're serious about changing your life for the better, then it's your job to manage your ego and to keep its executioner in check. I get so sad when I talk to people and they tell me, "One day I will start my own business, be an author, be a speaker, help others…," but they never follow through. I see (especially) women get stuck in the big fear of making a *wrong* decision. At the same time, they fail to realize that making no decision is *also* a decision. A decision *against* following your dreams and living a life on purpose, standing in your truth, and greatness. Just because you're not actively saying "no" to it, every day procrastinated is a day you choose safety (fear) over fulfillment (essence).

And I get that.

We've all procrastinated for some time. It's not like we throw our lives out the window on a hunch. And I also know that sometimes it can feel overwhelming to create a new life based on new rules. It can be terrifying to feel like you have a much bigger role to play, but at the same time have no idea how to make it happen or if you're even good enough. I've been there. Your purpose will most likely take you in front of your biggest fears…

may it be speaking, writing, teaching, leading, giving up safety. But that doesn't mean you shouldn't do it. It means there's a lot of potential for you to grow into! And always remember, when you're called to do it, you *CAN* do it. You'll meet the right teachers, coaches, people, and opportunities that will guide you.

But what if you're off, when you try? Well, what would be worse for you in the long run: the pain of being worse off or the pain of wondering how grand your life could've been if you had ever really tried? Remember the number one of the dying according to Bronnie Ware's book: "I wish I'd had the courage to live a life true to myself, not the life others expected of me." Enough said.

The Divine truth is that fear cannot prevail where love is present. You can either feel love or fear. Love is always stronger than fear. When you shift your perspective in those fearful moments toward serving yourself and others, the whole picture changes and with it your emotions. See the good that will come from your actions before it has happened. Hold to the positive vision and tell your ego, "Thank you for pointing out this risk. But your services are not needed right now. I got this."

Courage Mindset:

- Acknowledge your fears and know that they're part of the ego. The ego can only reign if you let it. When you push fear away, it only becomes stronger. The path is to move through it.
- Manage fear instead so that you can make independent, informed, and clear decisions.

93

- Be aware of the moments when your ego kicks in and wants to stop your success instead of supporting it.
- Trust that you are reading all this for a reason and the reason is, you're ready to overcome any fears and create your most amazing life.

Courage Mastery:

- List at least three situations in your life where you felt intense fear, but you did it anyway. Describe the situations thoroughly. Why were you scared? Why did you do it anyway? What did you learn about yourself in these situations? How did you feel afterward? What had changed for you? Be specific.
- List at least three situations when you were a big/small hero, either for yourself or others. What happened? How did you help? What gave you the strength? Be specific.
- What was the biggest struggle in your life? How did you overcome that struggle? What kept you going? How did you figure it out? Explain in detail.
- Want to use the free bonus workbook I created for you? This way please: sharonkirstin.com/bookbonus

Pledge #5

Vision

Finding your authentic truth and living an empowered life is a beautiful process. Most of us embark on this journey only with a feeling of longing and desire for more of life for us and people around us. Usually we don't wake up one day and have a grand vision of what our life will be and the action plan to follow through. Probably discovering your purpose and creating a life based on your own truth, is so rewarding because you're *not* given an outline of how to do it, but it's on you to find your unique path. There is no "how-to tutorial" on YouTube that will tell you *your* truth and purpose in life. Yes, there is guidance on how to find it in yourself, just like the book you're reading, but you have to do the work. You have to show up for your mission every day.

The only way you can stay motivated to reach a better life, is to be 100 percent clear on what a better life means to you. Your heart's and soul's desires are accurate pointers in the direction of your purpose. They show you what is possible for you. The phrase, "A dream is a wish your heart makes" is corny, but it's true. Whatever you feel in your heart is meant for you; it *is* meant for you. You can trust this guidance. You don't have to talk it down or silence it. Not anymore.

Many people I work with feel that they are meant for something big. But of course, their ego jumps in and says, "Who are you to be grand? Who are you to teach? Who are you to do what you love? Look, here, here, and here; you don't have it figured out. Nobody will listen to you anyway!" Maybe you've had that internal dialogue before, but your heart's desire became stronger, your soul's screams got louder, and you can't help but start inquiring about what your purposeful place can be.

Reconnecting to your soul's vision for you will help you keep a clear focus on how you want to live, feel, what you want to do, and who you want to be. It's your North Star that you are continuously sailing toward no matter how rough the sea gets around you. You won't let the waves brushing up on your ship keep you from holding a steady course. Fear won't stop you. Detours won't stop you. Roadblocks and even setbacks won't be able to affect you because you know what is meant for you. You've seen it, you want it, you can already feel it in your bones. It's *yours* and all you have to do is keep reaching out your hands until you can grab your star out of the sky.

Vision Mindset:

- Create a compelling and authentic vision of your better life and understand *why* this is what you desire.
- Define success on your own terms (it may differ to what you believed until now).
- Understand that better isn't always better, more isn't always more — keep letting go of the societal conditioning and reconnect to your truth.

Vision Mastery:

- Make a list of all your dreams. Don't censor; free write about it as long as you're in the flow. Just thinking about them won't have the same effect. Feel free to use the interactive workbook I created for you to give you structure: sharonkirstin.com/bookbonus

- *Why* do you desire your dreams? Ask why until you're at the core of the desire. For instance, the why for wanting to be rich is never money or shiny things, but it's an emotional need it will satisfy like safety, opportunity, freedom, or contribution.

- If there were no limits and no consequences, what would you do, be, and have? Be unrealistic here — no limits, no consequences...

- Is there someone you're doing this for? Your kids, family, or partner maybe? How will their life be better if you follow purposeful success? Can you draw motivation from this? How? Why? Be specific.

Pledge #6
"Shit Sandwiches"

You've dreamed big and yes, you should reach for the stars! It's not going to be a ride on the rainbow all the way. If you decide *for* something, at the same time you decide *against* something else. If you choose one partner, you are basically saying no to all the other men on the planet. Sometimes the partner you choose comes with bad habits, right? Highly unlikely that it's the perfect version of the man you'd bake for yourself. Yet, and this is the important part, the aspects you don't like are outweighed by the ones you love. For instance, you can live with him being late most of the time because you love how he supports you.

The same goes for living your purpose. You will have to do some things that you don't enjoy. The question for you is, do you love the thing you want to be, do, and have *enough*, that you'd endure the thing you dislike? Even if it's just for a while?

The other day I was watching an interview with Elizabeth Gilbert, the author of *Big Magic* and she put it into brilliant words, "Finding your true purpose is about deciding which flavor of shit sandwich you are really in for."

I'll tell you the truth, when I said I'd figure this whole purpose thing out, I went cold turkey. I was fed up and I couldn't go to my life-sucking job one more day. I quit. I didn't transition smoothly. Nada. I've always been a bit radical in my decisions, so it was authentic to me.

But oh gosh, the shit sandwich that came with it! I had to deal with the pressure of not yet knowing what I'd do next. I had no real idea what my gifts were, my purpose, or even how I was going to make money. It was a tough time for me because people told me I was committing "corporate suicide" and at the same time, I had nothing "better" to show for it. Even worse, I was turning on a spiritual path and I felt scared that the people from my past would label me crazy because I communicated with angels and started giving energy healings. It didn't end there. The shit sandwiches kept coming in the form of insecurity, fear, rejection, failed product launches, shifting business models, attracting clients that weren't a good fit, having to reassess my business model and message countless times, and investing a large five-figure sum into trainings and coaching.

And with every decision, every rejection, and every time I had to get back up, I had to take a long, hard look in the mirror and ask myself: *Do I still want to do this? Do I like the flavor of my shit sandwich?*

My answer has always been yes, no matter how desperate and pressured I felt. I have vision beyond my current circumstances and I know I am supported on this journey. The same is true for you. You can have your dream life, if you're willing to eat the "shit sandwich" that comes with it.

"Shit Sandwich" Mindset:

- Keep in mind — you'll be served a shit sandwich. Plan ahead on whether you'll be willing to eat that particular flavor when you choose your route.
- Keep moving ahead, even if you experience a small failure along the way. We all do. That's okay.
- Know that not everything is going to be great just because you follow your truth. There will be opposition. People will try to talk you out of it. Your ego will try to talk you out of it. Stay true to yourself and follow your heart.

"Shit Sandwich" Mastery:

- What is the shit sandwich that comes with your dream? Maybe there's more than one. Is it insecurity, a temporary loss of safety, no guarantees, criticism, rejection, discomfort, or something you don't like to do? Write it down and be specific.
- If you'll get what you love, are you willing to eat the shit sandwich as long as it takes?
- What if there was no guarantee that you'll get what you desire, would you still eat it?
- Make a list of pros and cons of following a path of purpose. You don't have to know the exact end goal yet for this exercise. Just look at the path you'll need to walk — what are the pros and cons of walking it? Be specific. This will give you a first idea where you are on the readiness scale.

Pledge #7

Inspired Action

What will you do one day when the timing is right? Nothing. The timing will *never* be *right*. There's never the right time to have a baby, start a diet, or follow your dreams.

You need to *decide* at some point in time that you want the dream, baby, purpose, or healthy body *now*. Waiting for some magic incident to grant you permission is just not how you'll ever make your dreams come true. I'm quite sure you're an achiever. You're ambitious in many areas of your life, especially those that are seemingly more important than others. For instance, let's say advancing in your career is important to you; the demands on your time and energy are high. Yet, feeling happy and loved in a relationship is also important to you, but you'd have to actively put focus on it and manage this area to reap rewards. We can't put all areas of our life to priority number one on our list, and often the more intangible, less urgent topics get pushed aside to a time and space when the timing is right. Again, that's never. We do it unconsciously though, and at one point in our lives, we wake up and realize we're a forty-two-year-old woman with an unfulfilled child wish and no partner. (If you're not a woman, you get the picture right?) Of course, there are still opportunities, but is that how you desired it to be? Is this the experience that your soul desires? I don't know! Your call.

My point is: If we don't prioritize our purpose, it will *never* come true. That's a fact. It's uncomfortable to admit it, but if you're not willing to go for your purpose and dreams now, you never will. Timing will never be more convenient than it is now.

Without action, your purpose stays an indefinite dream, the idea of a child that will never be born onto this colorful planet. It can never thrive or touch anybody's life positively. Not even your own.

Action Mindset:

- Schedule time regularly that you'll spend creating your purpose. It may be meditating on it, meeting like-minded people, or going through the exercises of this book. Make time for it so that clarity and progress can come to you.

- Take it from Tony Robbins: "Never leave the site of a decision without taking action." Take a first step in the moment of making a decision — call someone, book something, do something. Whatever it is, show the Universe that you're serious about your purpose and that you're showing up for it.

- Always take scary action toward your dreams and watch the miracles unfold. The Universe always comes halfway to support you!

- Once you've made a decision, stick with it. It's proven that successful people make decisions fast and they are slow to change them, whereas less successful people are slow in finding decisions and change them often.

Action Mastery:

- Take out your cell phone and make appointments with yourself. Dedicate time to finding and living your truth. Right now.

- What decision can you make right now that will lead you closer to your purposeful life? What's the action you're willing to take right now that accompanies it?

- What would be the most scary action you can take today or this week (within reason — don't go out and quit your job if it's not the right time to do so) to move you more into your truth?

- When did you take a scary action toward a desire? Explain what happened and how it served you.

- Practice taking action based on your intuitive feelings. Does your intuition/gut tell you yes or no? Begin asap to train this (maybe) new muscle. It will serve you greatly in all areas of your life.

Pledge #8
Faith

Soon you'll create your own relationship with the Supreme. It's essential for this sacred journey because it amplifies faith in a higher intelligence. Faith is important for two reasons.

Released Pressure: With faith that an infinite intelligence that encompasses all consciousness in the cosmos is guiding you toward your highest good and the highest good of everyone involved, it takes a huge chunk of performance pressure off your chest. You can relax into the knowing that you're guided. You can receive the gifts from the Universe openly. You trust that you are moving toward the realization of your dreams no matter the outward experiences. With faith, you can believe that they are already yours and they are on their way to you. In full faith, you speed up the manifestation process. You align with your purpose and it will come to you through people and other physical channels. Divine timing is at play in this Universe. The next step on your path will always show when you and everyone else is ready to deliver. In full faith and trust, while you're taking intuitive action, your desires manifest in Divine timing without pressure, fear, or anxiety.

Playfulness: The second reason is that faith in a higher power makes this journey less of a chore. It is not a chore. It's not the same path you took to go to school, study, find a job, and work hard. There is no linearity and there is no "must." Your life is not a chore or a burden. It is a gift of self-realization. You can try and fail and be fully open to all that earth offers. Rejoice in the emotions, experiences, people, and wild adventures on your path. Finding and living your purpose is a sacred journey that can be playful and fun if you have faith that you are fully guided and held along the way.

For a long time, I'd been clinging to the old way of doing things. I was so used to pushing things into being through willpower and discipline that I tried the same when I started walking my path of truth. That's a recipe for failure, disappointment, and disconnection from your source power. I've tried it; it's painful and slow.

Your purpose journey will move at the pace of your readiness. It'll move as fast you clear your inner world so that the outer world can adjust to your new energy signature. The law of resonance is always accurate. If what you're seeing around you is not what you desire, you need to change the inner programs that still resonate with it.

Infinite Intelligence will guide you forward always presenting you with the *next* lesson for you to move ahead. With faith in Divine timing and your higher guidance, you can stay playful and relaxed on the path. Don't push, don't hurry.

Your purpose will carry you at some point — financially, emotionally, energetically — and that is our goal. But don't burden the process from the beginning with huge expectations and responsibilities. The less you expect, the sooner it will come. Fear stops you; faith accelerates you.

Faith Mindset:

- Remind yourself that you are part of the essence of the Universe. It will always support and guide you, and has nothing but unconditional love for you. It cheers you on to be your most authentic self.

- Relate yourself to Spirit in a harmonious way to feel the support. Start by being grateful for everything you already have. I'll show you more in the next chapter.

- Write down at least three instances in which you had (or could've had) complete faith because it turned out fine without you having to obsess over it.

Faith Mastery:

- Write an affirmation or reminder that you choose to have fun finding and living your purpose and hang it in your home. Intentions are important because they will determine your experiences. You want it to be hard? You can have that too.

- Notice in which situations you're trying to control the how or the outcome. Being a control freak shows that you have zero faith. Write down at least three areas of your life where you control too much (successfully or unsuccessfully). Why is it hard for you to let go? What are you afraid of? Is it true? Who would you be without that thought? What would be a new empowering thought? Be specific and write it all down.

- Trust more. Have faith that even without your control, things will unfold beautifully. How can you have more faith in the three areas you mentioned above? Can you even give some tasks to someone else and trust that even though they won't do it just like you, it will get done well? Write it down!

- Make a request to the Universe. Start with something small that you feel is completely possible to receive. Feel how it would feel to already have it. Let the emotion flood your whole body and then release it to the Universe. Forget that you asked and take intuitive action (no matter how illogical). Have faith that it is coming to you. Just like you'd have complete faith that a letter will be delivered once you put it in the mailbox.

- Here's the URL to the free workbook again, if you'd like to use it: sharonkirstin.com/bookbonus

Pledge #9

Money Mindset

I didn't think I'd list this as a separate challenge, but we're so wrongly conditioned about it that I think it will serve you. For some, using the term money in the context of purpose feels dirty. As if it's tainting some of the sacredness of this journey. If you feel this way, well my darling, this is for you…

Money is not more or less than energy. It holds a frequency just like you, me, and everything else in the Universe. Money is not good or bad. Money is only a tool. Yet a very important one for your purpose. On our planet, we use money to trade products and services. That's all there is to money.

Now, the only thing that can be labeled good or bad about money is what *people* do with it. Money is *not* the problem but the *people* using it. People can be mean, dysfunctional, cruel, dirty, or greedy. Money can't. It's just paper that holds a certain frequency. If we had chosen bananas as our tool for trading, then bananas would be dirty. But it does seem quite strange to blame the banana for how a person uses it. The banana has no will of its own. So it would be ridiculous. Agreed so far?

Money is loaded with disempowering beliefs. Through societal conditioning, we all have given money a personality (whether you know it or not) and we've labeled our relationship with it good or bad. It's not the money's fault. It hasn't done anything wrong. It's just serving its trading purpose. How money reacts to you is based on your money mindset. (Law of resonance, remember?)

Many people feel that following their purpose may lead them into poverty. They could never make money doing what they love. Some feel as it's shameful to ask money for their gifts given from the Divine. I get that a lot. And I've been there too.

It's not holy to sacrifice yourself for others. It won't make you a saint. It's an action against the increase of life for all. Being broke, miserable, depleted, and unable to serve your Divine purpose is a disservice to all of life.

Think about it, who do you think can help more people and make a bigger impact in this world: the rich person who shares her wealth or the poor person who barely survives?

The problem is, we've been conditioned with a belief that rich people have bad character, they're selfish, greedy, and always taking from others for their own gain. Sure, there are people like that out there, but that wouldn't be you. Just because you value money for the freedom, opportunities, and contribution you can give through it doesn't make you greedy. Asking for no money in return for your services doesn't make you a better person. It makes you a person who will struggle, fight to survive and with it, forget about your purpose.

Remember that Spirit wants to express itself through you fully. For you to be more, know more, and do more, you need to *have* more. Your desire for more in life is the essence of the Divine urging you to use all the beautiful resources available to you.

*"Life, by living, multiplies itself. It is forever Becoming
More; it must do so, if it continues to be at all. We are
subject to the urge of life, seeking expression, whichever
drives us on to know more, to do more and to be more. In
order to know more, do more and be more we must have
more; we must have things to use, for we learn, and do,
and become only by using things. We must get rich,
so that we can live more."*
— Wallace D. Wattles

View the money you make from living your purpose and
serving others as a win-win. You are increasing their life through
your gifts while you are also increasing your life. By increasing both
your lives, you allow that which you are made of (source) to live
more fully in both of you. You both can thrive and serve more and
with it increase the lives of yet again many more.

There is no lack of money (or anything else) in this Universe.
There is enough for everyone to get rich if they understand the
science and art of using the Universal laws. Riches do not come
from competition but from creation. Following your purpose
makes you manifest from the creative plane of Spirit. There is no
competition. Nobody will beat you to *your* purpose.

Money allows you to take care of you so you can continue
serving. It can also enable you to expand your reach and make an
even bigger impact. Money gives you the means to recharge your
energy, hire people who can support you, and give you the space to

be creative. A positive relationship with money is like a partner who will always have your back.

Money Mindset:

- If money was your partner, what would your relationship be like? Describe both sides and be specific.

- How would you like it to be instead?

- Are there times when you are turning money away or are having a hard time receiving? For instance, deflecting compliments, not accepting your friend's invite, not accepting gifts. Be specific.

- Make a list of all the limiting beliefs you've been told growing up. For instance, "Money doesn't grow on trees," "Save money for a rainy day," and so on.

- Now pick the ones you feel most strongly about and start turning them around into empowering statements. For instance, "The Universe's abundance is flowing to me" or "Money takes care of me." Whatever feels right for you. But pay attention to make it a positive, truly empowering statement and notice how it feels in your body when you say it.

- What is your first memory around money? What belief was shaped back then? How is this belief still active in your life? Be specific.

- What's your mother's relationship with money?

- What's your father's relationship with money?

- Looking at their relationship with money, what did you copy and learn from them?

- Now that you know your old money story, write down your new money story. Define your new relationship. Be specific.

- Here's the URL to the free workbook again, if you'd like to use it: sharonkirstin.com/bookbonus

Money Mastery:

- Write the positive money statements on paper and hang them in your home to be reminded.

- Make it a habit to speak them out loud as affirmations every day.

- Come up with three ways to improve your relationship with money.

- In which instances will you be conscious of your attitude and open to receiving more? It may be money, compliments, invites, help, etc.

- Remember the new money story you decided for yourself? Make it come to life by *being* that new person! Writing it down won't make a difference; step into the new energy and live it! Notice the different outcomes every time you act out your new money story.

"Your time is limited, so don't waste it living someone else's life. Don't be trapped by dogma — which is living with the results of other people's thinking. Don't let the noise of other's opinions drown out your own inner voice. And most important, have the courage to follow your heart and intuition. They somehow already know what you truly want to become. Everything else is secondary."

— Steve Jobs

CHAPTER 4

YOUR SOUL'S PURPOSE & POWER

"At the center of your being you have the answer;
you know who you are and you know what you want."
— Lao Tzu

Time to reconnect with your essence! In this chapter, I'll take you through a series of structured exercises and meditations that will lead you into closer contact with your soul essence and purpose. This is where the rubber hits the road. Now you can create gentle, yet deep transformation in yourself, your life, and step ahead to live your purpose.

I've structured the steps so they build on each other. The first time you move through the content, it's best to stick with the flow. I hope this book and the tools in it will become your companion on the path to living your most authentic life, so use it as your intuition guides you. I know you a have a lot going on in your life and often we don't make time for what isn't urgent right now. Just remember that finding your truth and living a life that fulfills you *is urgent.* Your soul has guided you here; it's not an accident or casualty. It's the mystery of life guiding you to embark on this sacred journey of finding your purpose so you can live a fuller, happier, more energetic and impactful life. If you ever feel unmotivated or "fall off the wagon" during the journey, read step five on taking action.

I believe in discipline and I believe we all need to manage our time and energy in a way that our priorities are met and we're moving toward our heartfelt goals. Yet, when we love something and it brings us meaning and joy, I also believe we'll be intrinsically motivated to get more of it, simply because it touches our soul and makes us feel good. This is what I hope this journey of realigning with your truth will feel like for you.

A few recommendations on how to set yourself up for success, if you are serious about living your purpose, truth, and full potential as soon as possible.

✓ **Set an intention:** How do you want this process to unfold? What do you want most help with? How do you want to feel? What insecurities or worries would you like to let go of? What do you want to discover or reconnect with? Do you want to have a business idea? Or do you desire guidance on how to best transition to a new job? The Universe works based on intention. The intentions we set steer us on a course of manifestation. The Universe takes your intentions and creates the "how" around it. The clearer you are about what it is you want to achieve, the easier the Universe can support you in miraculous ways.

✓ **Schedule time:** Make a decision right now that you will make time for the exercises in this book. Notice how I didn't say when you will *have* time. I consciously said *make* time because it is your responsibility to choose the time in your schedule. The first rule to make yourself follow through on anything that's important is to schedule the time in your calendar and keep showing up. This is an appointment with your soul, with your creator. You are not going to be alone during these hours. The Universe is watching you and will determine whether you are committed based on the effort *you* put in. So, open the calendar on your phone right now and make a commitment. Once a day, twice a week — you decide how fast you move through this content. Just remember, the Universe invests just as much energy into supporting you, as you put effort into supporting yourself in this process. It's in your hands.

✓ **Trust the process:** The worst thing I hear smart people say is: "Oh, I've done this before; I don't need to do it again." Or "I've tried it, it didn't work." This is when intelligent people throw stones in their own path and make progress impossible. It's also what differentiates the high achievers from the doers. People who are constantly raising their standards know that doing a similar exercise just a few months or maybe even weeks apart will still open up new dimensions of insight. The answers change depending on who you are in that moment. You are embarking on a transformational process right now, so who you are now will vary greatly from who you are after finishing this book. Even if you've done some of the exercises before, do them again now.

✓ **Repeat the process:** This being said, you can go through the journey multiple times at different stages on you path. I'd love for you to see this book not as a one-off read, but rather as a study guide that travels with you. When I started treating transformational books like tools to retrain the way I think and act, it made all the difference. I could finally retain information and change my way of thinking and being. That rarely happens when you read through a book once and have huge gaps in between each reading session.

✓ **Use it for guidance:** When you're feeling challenged in your life, job, or relationships, take this book as an oracle. Take the book in your hands and hold it against your heart. Ask a question, for instance, "What are the best next steps for me to achieve xyz?" or "What is blocking me from xyz?" or "What do I not see in this situation?" You can ask anything with the intention to get a clear answer from the book. Then put your finger on the cursor at the bottom of the screen and let your intuition guide you to a spot along the scale. In a physical copy of the book, use your thumb to browse through the pages and stop where your intuition guides you to. Then look up at the page and notice where your gaze rests. Read the first sentences you see. Trust that this is a message for you that will give you clarity and guidance. Take a moment to understand how it relates to your current situation. Follow the guidance.

✓ **Get support:** If you haven't yet, make sure to download your exclusive and free workbook at: sharonkirstin.com/bookbonus. It will help you stay organized and on track with your progress.

Step #1

Discover Your Truth

"Knowing others is intelligence; knowing yourself is true wisdom. Mastering others is strength; mastering yourself is true power."

– Lao Tzu

Just because you feel the desire to make a change in your life doesn't necessarily mean you know exactly where you're heading. I know I had no clear idea of what I would end up doing when I ditched corporate. I also didn't have a mentor to help me figure it out, so it took me way longer than it needed to. My hope is that my lessons learned will serve you so your path to purpose is a lot smoother, clearer, and less stressful.

Two major truths for you to remember throughout your journey:

1. What you desire, desires you just as much. Probably more.
2. Your desire is already yours. You are not living, doing, or being it yet, only because *you* are in resistance to go get it or receive it. Nobody is keeping it from you.

This is so important. Listen up; all the doors are open and limitless support is available to you to reconnect with your truth and live a life that excites your soul. If anything, the Universe is cheering you on to become all that you can be. It has been patiently waiting for the moment you decide to step up and own your truth.

> *"Your task is not to seek for love, but merely to seek*
> *and find all the barriers within yourself*
> *that you have built against it."*
> *— Rumi*

I love this Rumi quote, and when you substitute the word "love" for "purpose" or even "essence," it gives you an exact message. The Supreme, which means *all that is*, is ultimately love. You are seeking love, the love within you that you come from, that you're a part of. It is not a fight or struggle to live your essence or even to find it. It is a homecoming and realignment of energy that will feel natural to you. Staying off course is the struggle. Forcing things to happen that aren't meant for you is a struggle. Living in flow with your essence is easy, nurturing, and heart-opening. It's like a sigh of relief once you snap back into alignment.

The question is then: What has kept you from following your heart, living your truth, and fulfilling your purpose?

Ego's Direction

Why do we detour so much from our true heart's desires? Why does it seem to be so hard to know our truth and follow our dreams?

Remember the distractions that we've been given by creation to make it more of a challenge to remember our soul essence, who we *really* are? It's part of the game to be blind to the other side of the veil. The mind, ego, and fear are masters in detouring us from our soul's purpose. Not because they are evil, but because it's their job to keep us safe. To the ego it's not safe to admit change or growth into your life. It can't control changes, and if it can't control the situation, it can't guarantee your safety and ultimately your survival. The soul, on the other hand, knows that change and growth are necessary for you to remember your essence. The soul is comfortable with change. It rests in the serenity of faith and trusts in a higher power because it knows it is — you are — part of that higher power. It is always safe.

The ego lives in the mind. Your soul and truth live in the heart. What have you been trained to listen to and act upon? Logic or feelings? Aren't feelings often discarded as fleeting notions of irrationality that we can't rely on? Well, the main problem is that often we can't distinguish between the emotions we feel and deep, heartfelt truths that originate in our soul because the ego is throwing a tantrum. Only few of us had role models that guided us to follow our heart. Most of us had parents and teachers who believed that education and a steady job were the best way for you to go. And I'm not saying it's not. I'm just saying a standardized path *may* not make you happy.

Your mind has been given the prime role in making decisions in your life. I'm sure it has led you down a path that is secure and successful, but you're reading this because something is missing. Let's dive deeper...

Your mind doesn't react new to each current circumstance. No. It remembers everything that has *ever* happened to you and draws upon this knowledge to make cross-references to the situation at hand. It has been taught what to be afraid of, what to avoid, and what to create more of. The good and bad experiences you've had have all been stored within your subconscious mind. Past experiences are saved for future reference so that you don't get hurt or killed and react faster in dangerous situations. Remember Bimbo, the baby elephant? Conditioned. In his mind, the failed attempts to break free created a belief that he is not strong (enough). We both know he is. But he doesn't. So he stays in his old ways of action and reaction.

The same happens in your life. You have endured tough situations as a child and teenager, maybe even later in life, that have created belief-systems in you. You've endured pain that you never want to feel again and your subconscious found a way to protect you.

Your first and strongest conditioning happens in early childhood. As an innocent baby, you need your parents to love you so that your survival is guaranteed. After all, if *they* don't love you, who will? Who will protect and nurture you? Chances are, no one else. Good thing nature created the hormone oxytocin so that we'll love our newborns unconditionally. The older you get though, the more you need to adapt to stay part of the team. You need to fit in and do something to be loved. Being adorable (thanks, oxytocin) isn't enough anymore. All this doesn't happen consciously, obviously.

After all it's the parents' job to make a decent human being out of you so you know how to survive and thrive on your own. They pass on their best knowledge to you. From early on, you soak up beliefs, habits, and character traits from your family. You take on beliefs about worthiness, love, relationships, money, food, body image — you name it! You copy behaviors without filter because that's all you know at an early age and you trust that it's true.

There are three tricky aspects to this:

1. **Well meant, but disempowering**: The best knowledge from your family doesn't mean it's *empowering* knowledge or even objectively true. Your family members have had their own trauma, drama, and experiences that shaped their thinking. Often parents want to keep us from making the same mistakes they did so they imprint us with "positive beliefs." They mean well, but often the beliefs impose limits to our power rather than its expansion.

2. **Three-year-old calling the shots**: Your own experiences shaped you at an early age. Ever since you were born, you came up with strategies to survive. You had to. But not all of these beliefs are empowering for you now. Yet, these early conditionings have become so much of who you are that often you don't even recognize that you are *now* acting based on beliefs that a three-year-old kid came up with.

3. **We believe that's who we are**: Unless we are self-aware and on a path of personal growth, we just never question the validity of the beliefs, fears, and habits that we display.

It has become our character, our identity. We accept that this is who we are as a person. We are fearful. We are shy. We are ambitious. But there is a reason, a conditioning, for everything we are. I dare you to question the truth of these invisible calls to action and instead *create* who you desire to be now.

Here's an example of how this works: let's say that a man had a baby girl. He wanted her to have the same standing in society that his son could get. He envisions a great education and well-paying job for her so she can have a good life. His conditioning says that will be the best for her. So he has high expectations for his girl and continuously teaches her about the importance of education and getting a well-paying job. The girl, like all kids, desires love from her parents more than anything in the world. The girl soon learns that she will receive love from her Dad in the form of praise, cuddles, or more time spent together when she succeeds. She brings home straight A's from school, is popular with friends, pretty, and well-behaved. The girl grows up to be a successful career woman with a well-paying job. Best in class, top performer, high standards for herself and others, overall successful.

That's great — Dad's childhood conditioning worked. He is proud and happy. She feels loved and like she's on the right path. After all, she fulfilled all the rules that were set for her life. The girl is a successful, independent woman now. Nothing wrong with that, right? Absolutely not, if it's aligned with the girl's soul and her inner calling.

Just think about it — when did Dad ever check in with the girl's desires? When did he ask her what she loved and what she felt she wanted to do? Did he give her space to find out what uplifts and excites her? Did he enquire about her passions and then brainstorm together what she could do for a living? Many parents don't. They trust the education system because it worked for them. Again, many of us are a new breed. We're change makers. The old systems don't satisfy us.

Now, this woman may be happy for a while. But then the excitement of achievement starts to wear off. She starts feeling unfulfilled, unhappy, hollow even. She has built her life on the childhood belief: "If I am successful enough, then I will be loved." At first it was the love of her Dad that she craved, but then it spread and it became a conditioned belief that she applied to everything — relationships, friends, colleagues, bosses. It soon became her standard of worthiness. It may even go so far that, unknowingly, she believes she doesn't deserve love and other good things unless she's put a lot of effort and sacrifice into "achieving" it.

The belief that was planted as a seed in childhood is not empowering. It's a disempowering belief based on lack. Her Dad was in a lack mentality when he decided that there was only one way his daughter could live a good life.

The truth is that she is worthy of love no matter what she does or doesn't do. No matter who she is or isn't. Yet, by following this belief, she feels compelled to recreate a reality day after day where she keeps fighting for approval and love. No matter what she achieves, it will never be enough. The fear of not being loved, if she doesn't get approval, is too big.

The interesting part is that these disempowering beliefs often become ridiculously funny once we become *aware* of them. This intelligent woman from our example knows that she won't be loved more by anyone just because she has a fancy title or more money in her bank account. Yet, the program is active in her subconscious mind and steers her to continuously behave that way. She's just not aware of it. She thinks that's simply who she is.

Have you seen the movie *Inception*? Probably you remember that Leonardo DiCaprio's character went into his wife's subconscious and changed a belief. Something she once knew to be true: the belief that the world is not real and she needs to wake up. That seed planted in her subconscious spread like a virus through her being and she was obsessed by it. It became her truth. It really wasn't the objective truth. But she believed it because she was conditioned to believe it. She went so far as to kill herself based on that belief.

It's a good way to understand this concept. What was planted as a seed in us and repeated over and over again as we were growing up becomes our truth. It's not an objective truth. It's our parents' truth. We may borrow their truth until we can create our own, but it's the responsibility of all of us to question our beliefs and plant our own truths.

Make it work:

- Whose approval did you crave more? Your father's or your mother's?
- Who did you have to be for him/her (to be loved)?
- Who could you never be?
- How does this translate to your life now? In which way does this still show up in your relationships, jobs, friendships, and overall behavior or feeling?
- What can you do differently to let this belief and behavior go?
- Do you recreate certain experiences over and over again?
- What is the common element and underlying belief?
- What can you do differently to let this belief and behavior go?
- Your life is a direct reflection of your internal world. What do you like? What don't you like? What belief is it rooted in?
- What beliefs did your parents, grandparents, or other influential family members imprint on you ever since you were young? Write down everything that comes to mind now, but stay open to discovering more and more each day.

Tip: There are many layers! A good question to continuously uncover hidden beliefs is "why do I want to / don't want to do this?" Keep asking why until you are at the root belief. Then evaluate if it is still serving you.

Soul Broadcast

Now you may be saying, "Okay, okay, I get that this conditioning thing is relevant, but what does that have to do with my purpose and soul essence?" Simple answer: everything.

What if, until now, you have interpreted your soul's guidance through a filter that didn't allow you to understand the messages clearly? Fact is, you are never cut off from receiving your soul's messages. You are your soul. You are your essence. In Divine truth there is no separation.

So, imagine a radio station signal. The signal at its source is crystal clear. But your radio may be tuned into the wrong frequency. How much of the broadcast can you understand then? Not much, right? You need to set your radio to the frequency at which the message is broadcast. How much will you understand then? You'll hear every word crystal clear, right?

Same goes for the message your soul is broadcasting to you. At the source it is crystal clear. Yet, we struggle to understand it. We're unsure how to tune back into source and hear the broadcast from the other side of the veil.

So what causes the distortion of the message? You may not (yet) be attuned to the frequency of the broadcast. The message is being broadcast and you can sense that, but all you hear right now is noise. Why are you in misalignment? Your mind holds on to countless conditioned beliefs. These beliefs are layered on your essence as filters. It's like layers of an onion. You interpret the crystal clear broadcast from your soul through countless filters that your mind created. As it comes to you layer by layer, the message is being altered by beliefs, conditioning, and fears; in the end, what you hear is only noise. It doesn't make sense. You're confused. Something doesn't feel right.

Your mind has no other way of understanding the message but by using its logic and conditioning to make sense of information. It uses what it has learned in this life (and past lives) to derive action steps. It is motivated by survival, safety, status, fear, and many other 3D illusions. The mind and ego are not to blame. It's part of the game. It's their job to keep up the illusion of separation, remember? Remembering your essence wasn't supposed to be for everyone.

Let's recap: you receive a crystal clear message from your soul about your purpose. You try to decipher it with your mind and ego kicks in and distorts the message into nothing but noise. Maybe you can get a few pieces of the message, but most of it is unclear and tainted by ego's fears.

The only way to bypass the false interpretations of the ego is to receive your soul's call where it originates: in your heart. Your heart has no filters and holds no beliefs. Your heart is the straight route to your soul, your true desires, and your ultimate potential.

When you let go of the need to listen to the ego, when you learn to manage it and put it aside, you can converse with your essence, Spirit, and the realms filled with light beings who are eager to help you.

When was the last time you listened to your heart without rectifying logically what it was guiding you to do? When was the last time you trusted your soul's guidance, your intuition?

Many of us have lost faith in the support of a higher power. We are running around trying to do everything out of our own human strength instead of calling on the mystical wisdom, guidance, and power of source energy. We burn ourselves out trying to do it all, have it all, and be all. We push harder when we feel resistance. We tell ourselves we are weak and not good enough if it doesn't work out the way we wanted. It doesn't even occur to us that our motives and goals may be out of alignment with our truth. We think we need to achieve a goal that we set our mind to no matter what.

Notice the important part of the sentence? *Set our mind to* versus *what our heart guides us to do*. Do you know the big difference between pushing to achieve a goal from the mind or a goal from the heart? When you are pushing toward achieving a goal originated in the mind, you can push yourself harder and harder and you'll get it. You adapt yourself to receive what you want. It is an outer journey. You focus on your goal and you move yourself there through stamina. You do whatever it takes, disregarding your inner guidance. Your focus is steadily fixed on the achievement of the outer goal. You've been trained your whole life to reach goals, so you know how to make it work. In the end, often you breathe a sigh of relief over what you have achieved. Finally! The struggle is over. But are you happier now? Often times, you don't feel different. Why? It's not aligned with your truth — it means nothing to you ultimately. So, you move on to a new goal and see whether that will fulfill you.

When you follow a heartfelt goal, you are also challenged, but you are challenged to become a better version of yourself. You do not set your sight on an achievement per se, but you know why you desire this goal. You are looking to create an experience, a feeling within yourself that you desire. It's first an inner journey to know what you desire and why. You face your resistance, fears, and desires within and you align yourself with your soulful goals. While you step ahead achieving, it you are becoming more and more of who you can be. You reconnect to yourself and your soul. You begin to feel stronger, more centered, more clear. In the end, you feel fulfilled with what you've created and who you've become in the process.

The path of the heart and soul is one of reconnection, inner strength, clarity, and transformation into all that you truly are. It leaves you stronger than you were before. Never weaker or burned out.

The further you progress on your path of purpose, the more your true self will come to light. The more you shed the veil of the ego and let go of limiting beliefs and disempowering stories, the more you are aligning yourself with *your* truth. Your truth lies in knowing who you really are. Your essence is pure truth. In the light of love, nothing else but the truth can prevail. The ego and fear are never the truth of who you are. Living from a place of truth means following what you feel and know in your heart is right for you.

You will need more courage, strength, and stamina to stand in your truth than to adjust your course based on what other people expect of you. As humans, we crave harmony; we need to be loved and we know we need to belong. We make many sacrifices to fit in, to be likable, to be how our family and society wants us to be. We think if we impersonate the stereotype of perfection we are guaranteed a "happily ever after." Those of us who make it this far know it's not true. Perfection is an unattainable standard. Wanting perfection or anything else that doesn't stem from your truth will always leave you more hollow than before.

"You can't connect the dots looking forward; you can only connect them looking backwards. So you have to trust that the dots will somehow connect in your future. You have to trust in something — your gut, destiny, life, karma, whatever."
– Steve Jobs

Make it work:

- What path have you been on until now? The path of the mind or the path of the heart? Explore this further — it may be a mix of both.

- If there were no limitations and consequences in any way, what would you be doing every day? What do you desire most? List all your desires and passions, down to the very details how you would express them in life.

- If there were no limitations and consequences, what type of life would you be living? How much would you "work?" Would you have a family? Would you travel? Who would you spend time with? What life would truly light you up?

Human Needs

Now that we're talking about what is true and important to you, it's the perfect time to introduce you to a concept from Tony Robbins. Tony became famous back in the day because he could recondition people within minutes. While going through one of his training programs, I picked up a concept that stuck with me right away, because it's *that* important.

Every person has six basic human needs. They are the same for everyone: certainty/safety, uncertainty/variety, significance, love, contribution, and growth. He explains that each one of us has two primary needs, the ones we are mostly steered by subconsciously. Not only do the six needs apply to your whole life, but also to every decision and experience in it. You'll always make a decision that will be based on the fulfillment of one of these needs.

There are countless systems on how to analyze yourself. That's not my goal here. I don't care about astrology, enneagram, palm reading, or any other system right now. They all have their relevance, but this is not one of these self-analysis systems that categorizes you. I'm sharing the six basic human needs with you because they will help you to connect on a more *intimate level with yourself*. It's not a system that imposes characteristics on you, but it's a way to get to know yourself better and understand what triggers you to think and act a certain way in any given situation. Priceless.

I'll explain the six needs in more detail, but let it be noted that I'm paraphrasing here and using my own words to describe them:

- **Certainty**: The need to feel safe. This could show up in a desire to stay in control of what's happening and especially the outcome you want to create. Making decisions with an uncertain outcome can be hard.

- **Uncertainty**: The need to experience variety in your life. This could be the desire to travel, see different cultures, take investment risks, have different partners, you name it.

- **Significance**: The need to feel important. This could be the desire to feel important to your family, certain people, or to the whole world. Often people who desire standing in society, a lot of money, or to impact others' lives, have a big need for significance.

- **Love**: The need to feel connected. Family, partners, and meaningful relationships are highly important.

- **Contribution**: The need to feel that you're giving back. This could be the desire to make the world a better place. You may feel like you can best help by contributing your gifts, parts of your income, or time.

- **Growth**: The need to feel like you are growing as a person. The desire to keep growing into more of your full potential personally, but also spiritually.

Each one of us has all of these needs, so you probably found aspects of each one within yourself. The interesting question is, how dominant is each one of these? And even more interesting: the importance of the needs can change in different situations in your life!

Let me give you an example to make it more tangible. Let's say Peter and George both have the goal of making one million dollars per year. Now, you could easily say they are the same, maybe even have the same needs. Well, we don't know yet. So, let's ask Peter why he wants the million bucks. Peter says that with the money, he can make investments, save, and reinvest in his business. He also wants his family to be safe and cares to contribute more to charity. George says his reason for wanting a million dollars is to travel, to have more freedom, and make a bigger impact with his work. One answer is not better than the other. So, their end goal is the same, but their reasons, the *WHY*, differs. Peter seems to be driven by safety and contribution. When these needs are met, he feels most fulfilled in life. For George, this wouldn't be right to live a happy life; his strongest needs that long to be fulfilled are variety and significance.

Another example: Many people have kids, but why did they want them? Probably it's a colorful mix of the six needs, but let's say for one parent, the most important need is to have love and connection with another human being. For the other parent, it is the need to grow as a person because she knew it would challenge her to be the best version of herself. Others may have kids to feel significant to at least one person on the planet or to give of themselves in a selfless manner. The outcome (having the kid) is the same, but the need that's getting fulfilled varies for each person.

Make it work:

- Look over the six basic human needs (certainty, uncertainty, significance, love, contribution, growth) and detect your two primary needs. The ones that are most important to you in life as a whole.

- How is your current life contributing to these two needs right now? This will be important to know once you decide to make a change. You'll be aware of why you may be attached to certain areas of your life more than to others.

- Why are you looking for your purpose in life? What need desires to be satisfied? What will a life on purpose give you: safety, variety, significance, love, contribution, or growth? What are the two key needs that purpose will satisfy?

- How can you make sure that the two most important needs will stay met while you transition from your current life into a life on purpose?

- Remember the life that you designed in the exercises above? Now, ask yourself *WHY* do you desire all this? It is not enough to know what you want — we're not chasing achievements or shiny objects here. For you to make sure you are living on purpose, you need to find the life conditions that will generate a *feeling* within you. Describe how the life conditions you desired above will make you feel.

- Is there a common theme or themes that seem(s) to be important to you? Freedom, joy, contribution, safety, variety, growth, love...? How is your current life contributing to them?

Identity

Who are you? Pure essence of love and light on a soul level? I love the way you listen, darling. But, for once, I'm not talking about that. I mean, who do you believe you are as human? What role do you play in our 3D game? What kind of person would you describe yourself to be? Kind, humorous, sensitive, ambitious, adventurous, rich, powerful, a giver, a taker, brilliant...?

Your soul carries experiences from many lifetimes that are still to some extent active. As soon as you dropped onto planet earth, you were conditioned by your family, friends, teachers, and mass media. You experienced trauma, pain, and drama. It all sums up to an interesting package of who you believe you are: your identity.

I've been talking so much about self-awareness and personal growth because it's so important to actively *create* your identity instead of living out unconscious conditioning. You can create the most powerful version of yourself or you can spend your life as the result of an unintentional mix of influences. I'm not saying anything about you is wrong. It's about stepping into all that you can be. If the unintentional conditioning created you as your most powerful version — hey, that's cool with me. But what are the odds? There is one big reason you need to know your identity and Tony Robbins said it best:

"The most powerful force in the human psyche is people's need for their words and actions to stay consistent with their identity — how we define ourselves."

If you believe you are a kind person, you will act kind and speak kindly to others. If you believe you haven't been given everything you deserve, then you will demand from others unconsciously. If you believe you can make anything happen, you will. If you believe everything you do fails, then you'll have a hard time trying to find motivation to do anything.

*"Whether you think you can, or you think you can't —
you're right."*
– Henry Ford

Make it work:

- Describe your personality, your identity in as much detail as you can. What do you believe to be true about yourself?

- Take ten minutes and write down the story of your life. You can also record it into your phone, but make sure that you spend the time to tell your story as if you were telling it someone else. Describe who you are, where you've been, what made you who you are today, why you made certain decisions, and how they made you feel in the moment and then down the road. Describe who you are and how you feel right now in your life. Where are you heading and how does that make you feel?

- Now that you see your own path a lot clearer, is this path still right for you? Why; why not? What parts are good; which ones aren't?

- It's time to write a new story. A few exercises ago, you wrote down or recorded your old story. You may or may not have been the victim in the story; there may have been things that were painful to experience. Now is your chance to recreate yourself. You can now design from scratch who you want to be instead. What's your story? What are your values? Who are you? Where are you going? What's important? Some aspects will stay the same and some will be new. Just give yourself space to think freely of who you desire to be if there are no limitations and consequences. Go!

- Write down at least ten of your truths. What do you know for sure? How can you use your truth to give you motivation and clarity on your path?

Summary Step #1:

- What you desire, desires you just as much. Probably more.

- You are not living your biggest life yet, only because *you* are in resistance to go get it or receive it. Nobody is keeping it from you.

- Your subconscious comprises ninety percent of your mind and influences your thoughts, feelings, and actions every moment of your life.

- It holds belief systems that are conditioned by your family, media, teachers, history, drama, and maybe even trauma.

Many of these beliefs may not be aligned with your truth and are ready to be reevaluated so you can access your authentic self, purpose, and potential.

- Your soul is broadcasting a crystal clear message about your purpose. You hear a lot of noise in the message because you are not attuned to the right frequency.

- You can attune to the frequency by letting go of the layers of false beliefs, fears, and ego.

- Your heart can receive the message without filters and bypasses the logic of the mind. Your heart essence is attuned to pure love, the frequency of the Universe.

- When you reconnect to your truth, you reach your soulful goals and are fulfilled with the outcome. You like who you become in the process.

- When you achieve goals that are not based on your truth, they often leave you hollow, burned out, and you quickly move on to a new goal.

- We all have six basic human needs: certainty, uncertainty, significance, love, contribution, and growth. We have two primary needs. These needs drive all of your decisions in life. Understanding what needs drive you helps to increase fulfillment in your life.

- Who you believe you are, your identity, determines your experiences. Humans have a deep drive to stay consistent with their identity, no matter whether this will lead to positive or negative outcomes.

- Through self-awareness and personal growth, you can actively *create* your identity instead of acting out unconscious conditioning.

Step #2

Realign with Your Talents

"You don't need to be better than anyone else;
you just need to be better than you used to be."
– Dr. Wayne Dyer

Awareness of the belief systems that brought you this far in life is a firm ground to build an even better life on. You've learned how to understand your own motives, needs, and internal programs. With continuous self-awareness of these programs, you can now drive positive change in your life. The next step is to get crystal clear on where you're headed.

You know, you're perfectly designed by the Supreme to fulfill a role that only you can fill. You have talents, gifts, and knowledge in a unique portfolio that is assembled perfectly for your purpose. Source knows you and it knows your every thought. You are never separated. It also knows how you can best contribute to the increase of all life.

In our army of light, we have different functions. Some are very skilled and naturally talented to be archers, others are in the cavalry, and others again are most potent in close combat. Then again there are healers who take care of the wounded, there are strategists, and there are those that we fight for. In this Universe, there is not too much or too little. Everything has purpose and nothing is wasted. Meaningful abundance is available to all of us if we tune into the flow of life.

Zone of Genius

You've been gifted with unique talents. No doubt. When you know your talents, you can share them with the world in a way that will contribute in two ways. One, you will live *your* fullest life that excites and fulfills you. Two, you'll contribute to the increase of life for others. Purpose is never one-sided; life fully expressed multiplies itself. Your purpose serves you *and* everyone who gets in contact with your gifts. You may heal, inspire, motivate, create, support, teach — there are endless ways, combinations, and topics in which you can increase life. The trick is to find what lights you up and design your life and work around it so that others benefit when they do business with you. Following your purpose is never selfish; it's selfless, because you contribute to us all.

Gay Hendricks wrote a powerful book called, *The Big Leap*. In the book, he makes the point that we all have four main operating zones:

- **Zone of Incompetence:** Activities you are not good at. Others can do them much better. Avoid these activities and delegate them because they only drain your energy.

- **Zone of Competence:** Activities you can do just as well as any other. You're not rising above the crowd, you're swimming with it. Don't dwell here; you won't be able to excel.

- **Zone of Excellence:** Activities in which you outperform others; you are more skilled than the rest. You are probably successful at what you do and tempted to believe that this is your sweet spot to work in. This is the type of job most of us in corporate are stuck in. You do your job well, you make a great living, you use some of your talents, you make profits for your company, but deep down, you sense that you're not living your full potential.

- **Zone of Genius:** Activities you are uniquely suited to do, that draw upon your special gifts and talents. When you operate in this zone, time ceases to exist and you can easily find yourself "waking up" hours later feeling blissful. Hendricks makes the point that when you live a life from your zone of genius, you will find satisfaction and fulfillment. (I agree.)

Your zone of genius could be something distinct and straightforward like speaking or painting, but you may also have a unique portfolio of gifts that make for a whole new profession. Sometimes it's not just black and white. But first, let's make sure you know your talents.

When I was working in corporate, I was living in my zone of excellence, although I didn't know it at that time. I thought my job was made for me because I could live out a variety of my gifts: creativity, design, coaching, optimizing websites, putting myself in the user's shoes (user experience), strategy, ambition, leadership — the start-up flair fed into my need of trailblazing, analytical thinking, and so on. There was really no shortcoming of the skills I loved using and am really good at. No wonder I felt like I was on top of the world. Yet, the nagging feeling of "there's something better," "there's more to life," wouldn't leave me.

For me, what was missing in the equation was contributing to a more meaningful outcome. Optimizing the user experience of online fashion shopping was great, but I didn't see that making a real positive impact on people's lives. I wanted to contribute in a more significant way and truly help people change their lives for the better. Now I'm still using all these skills; they are not obsolete, quite the opposite! The difference is that now I use them in my own purposeful business in a way that I draw tremendous fulfillment from them.

Following your purpose doesn't mean that everything you've done or achieved until now is obsolete. You may just reassemble it in a way that is more fulfilling to you.

Many people don't get intrinsically motivated to change their lives. Yet, I think more and more people in our generation *do* wake up and desire a better life. If you are one of them, high five! It's important to know though, that often our body has to do the heavy lifting to get us going on a path of purpose. When we get off course and our soul wants us to realign with our purpose, it sends signals, messages, people, anything it can, for you to realize that you're going down the wrong path. But, let's face it, often we just don't listen to subtle nudges. We don't trust that repetitive ideas and synchronicities are really signs for us to take action in a new direction. Change is still scary, isn't it? What trick does your soul have up its sleeve that will pull your attention? Your body.

Your soul will communicate through your body with you if you have ignored all the messages it sent before. You may get sick so that you start rethinking the way you've set up your life. It can be anything from a cold to a severe illness. Every time your body is not in complete health, it is trying to deliver a message to you. I hope you are reading this in full health and stamina, ready to tackle a new chapter in your life. If you aren't, know that you will feel better the more you realign with your purpose and essence. Health is your most natural state of being.

Make it work:

- What do you most love to do? List at least three things you can do over long stretches without getting bored.
- What work do you do that doesn't feel like work to you? List out all activities that come to mind and then list three more.
- What activities deliver the biggest output/abundance/fulfillment to time spent?
- List all the activities that you love at your current job (like I did above). Could you also be doing them in a different job setting?
- Define your zone of excellence in a short paragraph.
- Define your zone of genius in a short paragraph.
- Ask five people to tell you the five things they value most about you. This can feel vulnerable, but go out of your own way to do it. You can let them know you're reading this book and it would help you to get clarity on your talents.

Jazz Dance and X-Men

Let's travel back to your childhood. What did you want to be when you grew up? Try to remember all the professions you wanted and *why* you wanted them. This will give you a lot of insight on what your purpose is. This may need a bit of a Sherlock Holmes attitude though because it's not always straightforward. I remember that I had a hard time answering this question.

As a child I didn't have a dream job that I was going after. Sure, I wanted to be a famous singer or actor, but I never allowed myself to dream that big. I was even too shy to take singing lessons or to bear the anxiety of performing with my Jazz Dance Group.

Thinking back at *why* I wanted to be famous, it was never making music in itself. My *why* was to be an important inspiration for others, to make their life better, and to contribute with my gifts. As a young girl, the only way I could think of doing that was to model what I saw in the media: being a rock star. Another deep desire of mine was to have super powers (I never shared this with anyone before). She-Ra was my major role model back then. I loved how she transformed into her most powerful self by raising her sword and speaking the magic words, "For the honor of grayskull!" here are so many movies where heroes save the world with their super powers. While it wasn't an option to get some super-powered DNA strings like the X-Men, I later discovered where this longing came from. My search for purpose in life took me down a path of reconnecting with my own psychic and energy healing abilities.

While the dream of becoming a telepathic rock star who saves the world by stepping into her full potential seems a bit out there, it does make sense when I assemble the pieces now. Of course, I don't see myself waving up a sword like She-Ra or flying through the air like Superman. My dream is much more refined and grounded in my essence. I'm saving people in my own way by helping them heal and step into their full potential. I have reactivated my psychic gifts and connect to Angels, Goddesses, and other really cool light beings every day. I do throw up my imaginary sword and call upon my highest potential every day — to write this book, to create courses, to channel meditations, to serve my clients. I draw upon my higher wisdom and fuller potential in everything I do.

How about we look at your childhood dreams now? As a child, you didn't filter what you desired and what you dreamed of. You thought anything was possible. Your soul was speaking loud and clear.

Make it work:

- If you don't remember: Ask your parents what you wanted to be when you grew up. It may have changed through the years, so there may be different answers. Each one holds important information!

- *Why* did you want to be xyz when you grow up? Asking *why* will give you the answer you seek! It's the key to finding your purposeful answer. **Remember that purpose is not what you do, but who you are**. Take time to journal on the answer and reconnect with your inner child while doing so.

- What is the dream (no matter how unrealistic or vague it seems) that you carry within? *Who* is it you desire to be?
- How can you relate what you wanted to be and why you wanted to be that, to your current occupation?
- How can you take it a step further and brainstorm on possible new occupations that feed your soul essence? It may be your own business or a different job. Anything goes.

Lightshadows

Great job! Can you feel that you are getting closer and closer to the essence of who you are and why you came here? I'd like to finish this step strong, so I'll take you on an exercise that is very close to my heart. I do it regularly when I notice that I'm evolving, and I'm sure you'll love it as much as my clients.

Important:

Only read one bullet point at a time. The magic of this exercise unfolds gradually. If you read it all before doing the exercise, you spoil the transformational impact it can have on you.

You'll find the worksheet in the free workbook that I've created for you to accompany this book: sharonkirstin.com/bookbonus

Make it work:

- Take out a blank sheet of paper and divide it into three columns.

- On top of each column write the name of a person you admire.

- Now start filling in the columns with all the attributes you admire in them. Be as vague or as specific as you like. Write until there's no more to say.

- Stop reading, if you haven't followed through until now.

- Now, the important part: cross out the names of your role models and replace them with your name. Don't be shy. Do it. This is the magic of the exercise. Everything you see and admire in others is your own light. You have the same light within you, the same gifts and talents. You can do what you admire in others. You are made for this! They are a reflection of your greatness. The lightshadow is that you can't yet see it in you — your own light is hidden by your own shadow. It's a blind spot.

- Next, take your list and step in front of a mirror. Look into your own eyes and read all the attributes to yourself starting with "I am [attribute #1 from role model #1]," "I am [attribute #2 from role model #1]," and so on. Make sure you soak up the meaning of every word. You *are* this attribute already. It is within you and all you need to do is to own it, accept it, live it. Stop resisting the greatness of your essence.

the whole list as mirror affirmations to yourself.
t it every day if you like. Mirror affirmations prove
: more potent than affirmations spoken without
looking in your own eyes.

Summary Step #2:

- You're perfectly designed by the Supreme to fulfill a role that only you can fill. You have talents, gifts, and knowledge in a unique portfolio that is assembled perfectly for your purpose.

- When you know your talents, you can share them with the world in a way that will contribute in two ways. One, you will live *your* fullest life that excites and fulfills you. Two, you'll contribute to the increase of life for others. Purpose is never one-sided; life fully expressed multiplies itself.

- You have different zones of competency, and your zone of genius is the one where true fulfillment and purpose will be found.

- Following your purpose doesn't mean that everything you've done or achieved until now is obsolete. You may just reassemble it in a way that is more fulfilling to you.

- Often our bodies get sick to show us that we have gone off course on our path and that we need to realign with our truth.

- What you wanted to be when you grew up can hold important information on your purpose and desires.

Finding out why you wanted to be "that" will help you reconnect to your truth.

- You have a lightshadow that will give you exciting information about your purpose. Try the exercise!

Step #3

Surrender to Your Purpose

"When I let go of what I am, I become what I might be."
— Lao Tzu

Once we glimpse our purpose and full potential, our first impulse can be to get scared and jump back into what we know. We may be afraid of our light, our grandiosity, the limitless potential within us. When we see how we're made perfectly for our most exciting and fulfilling path, we also realize that we are fully responsible for owning our creator powers. It's a lesson in accepting that you're not the victim in life. It shows you that life is happening *for* you, in Divine synchronicity, never *to* you. Everything up until now has been orchestrated in a way that will give you the right growth lessons, experiences, and even trauma so you can serve in your biggest way. It is your choice to accept your purpose and the power that comes with it…or not. Then stay where you are.

"With great power comes great responsibility."
— Ben, Spiderman's uncle

When we want to crawl back into our hole, we tell ourselves our current lives are not so bad after all. We want to go back to a life that we've created over all these years with so much effort, time, and energy. Just think of all the costs we've incurred!

Just one problem with that: you've seen the mighty version of yourself. Nothing will be quite the same once you know who you really are. Any version of your life that doesn't honor your essence will be even more unfulfilling and bleak than ever before.

So, let's move forward courageously, shall we? This is a step of active surrender. We're trained to make things happen through massive action. This step will take courage because it means surrendering in faith that a higher power will carry you. Yes...letting go and falling into the arms of the Supreme so it can guide you to the biggest version of you and your life.

This was an utterly scary concept for me and I only realized the magic of it once I came to my breaking point. I couldn't push any further. My inner and outer pain seemed insurmountable. I gave up. Giving up is a no-no in our society, isn't it? We stamp people off as losers. That's why it took me so long to let go, but with it, I only delayed the magic.

You know, there is a difference between giving up when you should just push a bit harder and giving up your ego so a higher power can grab you and lift you to a purposeful path.

Let's remember:

- You're not on your most powerful path of purpose yet. Your soul has been screaming at you to make a move, but first you need to let go of resistance.
- Your purpose seeks you, as much as you seek your purpose. The layers of conditioning are just distorting the signal that will guide you there.

- You are part of the Supreme, part of all that is. The Supreme knows you inside out, every moment of the day. It watches over you with unconditional love and with the highest intentions for you and your life.

I think it's safe to say you are harboring a fair amount of mindset and energy that hasn't been helpful to make your life a masterpiece. Just like we all do. Consequently, it is best for your ego and mind to step aside so the Supreme can take over and guide you with clarity, ease, and grace into your purposeful life. Agreed?

This is going to be a short and sweet step, but a very crucial one. (Read: don't skip!) Take a deep breath and then speak out loud with heartfelt conviction:

"Dear Spirit/Supreme/God/Universe/Higher Self [enter your favorite term], I am now ready to follow a path of purpose. Please give me the courage, stamina, and crystal clear guidance, one that I cannot miss, to lead me into a life on purpose. Show me how I can best increase my life and the life of others, so that you can express yourself through all of us more. I herewith set the intention to fully accept, find, integrate, and live my purpose and full potential, in the most pleasurable, easy, financially abundant, and magical way. Or whatever better outcome you have in store for me. And so it is."

That's it. Your creator and the Universe always listens *lovingly*. It only loves. Please feel free to talk to Spirit and share your struggles and worries. You can adapt the statement so that it feels authentic to you. You could even start with something like "Dear Spirit, although I feel scared of what might happen next." or add words that are meaningful to you. Just be intentional and clear about it. The Universe is listening and will make it happen. You can always adjust. Just don't be surprised when what you ask for shows up in your life.

There is no need to repeat the statement. Speak it with an open heart and really mean it. This is it. Now watch the magic unfold. You will receive guidance, find yourself in synchronistic events, meet new people, come across information, and so forth that will guide you closer to your most fulfilling life and purpose in Divine timing.

Please be aware that Spirit loves you so much that it will give you the chance to go back. Changing your life and following a path of purpose is a commitment. Spirit will give you opportunities to go back onto your old path, just to make sure you still feel the same way and you didn't set the intention out of a fleeting emotion. In these moments, you may wonder if you're being guided to stay where you are. Know that you have the best guiding system within you: your heart. Ask yourself what the truth of the situation is — which decision is to your highest good? Restate the intention of purpose if you feel this is the right path for you and make it known to Spirit.

Knowing that you *will* receive these opportunities is a *big advantage*. You won't make any detours, unless you want to. There is no right or wrong path. You can make detours and you can set a new intention. Everything happens as fast as you'd like it to.

You may also start feeling different from others. Your friends or family may not understand your path, ambitions, or inner calling. That's okay. You are not here to transform them. Remember what is true to you, what you believe is right for you in that very moment. Only you and the Universe know the answer.

"Our deepest fear is not that we are inadequate. Our deepest fear is that we are powerful beyond measure. It is our light, not our darkness that most frightens us. We ask ourselves, Who am I to be brilliant, gorgeous, talented, fabulous? Actually, who are you not to be? You are a child of God. Your playing small does not serve the world. There is nothing enlightened about shrinking so that other people won't feel insecure around you. We are all meant to shine, as children do. We were born to make manifest the glory of God that is within us. It's not just in some of us; it's in everyone. And as we let our own light shine, we unconsciously give other people permission to do the same. As we are liberated from our own fear, our presence automatically liberates others."
– Marianne Williamson

Summary Step #3:

- Life is happening FOR you, never TO you.
- You are part of the Supreme, part of all that is. The Supreme knows you inside out, every moment of the day. It watches over you with unconditional love and with the highest intentions for you and your life.

- Surrender takes courage because it means surrendering in faith to a higher power.

- You will let go of your own ego and belief concepts and fall into the arms of the Supreme so it can guide you to the biggest version of you and your life.

- Surrender is the fastest route to purpose. Your mindset and ego have kept you on a detour all this time. They are disturbing influences on your path.

- The statement will be set with heartfelt intention so that the Supreme can get to work on supporting you.

- Spirit loves you so much that it will give you opportunities to go back onto your old path, just to make sure you still feel the same way and you didn't set the intention out of a fleeting emotion.

- You are in full control of how fast your life transforms into what you desire it to be.

Step #4

Master Your Energy

"The more you see yourself as what you'd like to become, and act as if what you want is already there, the more you'll activate those dormant forces that will collaborate to transform your dream into your reality."
– Dr. Wayne Dyer

Are you ready to move even further into the magic of you? If you aren't sure what your purpose is by now, don't worry, that's normal. It will gradually become clear to you. All the pieces are already coming together. You can be 100 percent certain that the Universe is already aligning opportunities, messages, and guidance. I love this about the Universe — it always meets you halfway. Your job is to stay alert and ready to see the messages, signs, and guidance that you are receiving based on your new intention to find and live your life purpose.

There are universal laws we all have to comply with. The law of gravity, for instance, but also the law of resonance, and the law of attraction. The latter are often misunderstood and ticked off as new age hocus-pocus. Well, I guess we humans have a tendency to ridicule (and fear) what we don't understand. Although these laws get a bad rap, they are accurate and they are working with you all day long. You are already using them, you can't opt out — just like you can't opt out of gravity. Otherwise, I'd already be flying like

Superman. Most people are just not using the law of resonance and attraction willingly and intentionally.

Quantum Field

I remember one particular meditation when I asked for clarity about my life purpose. Angels, Ascended Master, and Gods/Goddesses are always very present in my meditations and conduct healings, initiations, or give me visions of guidance. That day, I was worried I would get my purpose wrong. I was making changes in my business and I wanted to make sure that they were fully aligned with my purpose and soul essence. I set my intention for the meditation and dove right in. Not much later, Archangel Ariel appeared in a vision. Every angel has a specialty, and Ariel can support you in manifesting financial resources or paving the way for your life purpose. That day, she had very clear words for me that even today keep echoing in my mind:

"It's not about what you do, it's about who you are."
– Archangel Ariel

I never forgot these words and even wrote them in big letters on my vision board. This statement is not only true about purpose in itself, which is really about becoming the biggest version of yourself, but it's also true when looking at the laws in the Universe. Who you are, your energy field, attracts into your life what is aligned on a frequency level.

The quantum field does not respond to what we want;
it responds to who we are being."
— Dr. Joe Dispenza

Dr. Joe Dispenza has done enlightening neuroscientific research in proving how our thoughts and emotions can alter the quantum energy field around us and draw experiences from it toward us. His research shows that emotion combined with intention causes real changes in the quantum field. We are *that* powerful that we can change reality around us by pure emotion and intention. Mind-blowing, right?

Basically he proved that the law of attraction really works and put it in neuroscientific terms. Our brains love to get logical explanations, so if you crave yourself some of that good stuff, check out his books.

You probably know that you are 99.9 percent energy and only 0.1 percent matter, depending on whether you were listening in physics class or not. Although your body looks and feels pretty solid, on a quantum level it's not. This makes you a vibrating cloud of energy as part of a vibrating (quantum) energy field. This is the scientific explanation for why you are one with all that is. You are God/Spirit/Essence/Universe. You cannot separate yourself. Just to be clear, I often substitute the term "quantum field" and call it "the Universe/Spirit/Supreme/God/Infinite Intelligence." That's because they are all synonyms for the one all-encompassing source that we come from and are always part of.

If your energy is part of the field, it must mean that you are one with all that is. Separation is an illusion. As part of the universal field, you can alter the field as you wish through your thoughts and emotions. This again means that you are infinitely powerful and an active cocreator of your life.

Manifesting

Your energy has a unique electromagnetic signature. This signature resonates at a frequency (law of resonance) in the quantum field and draws from the field experiences, people, and things that are aligned (in resonance) with this frequency (law of attraction).

The most important question is, if you are constantly attracting (you can't stop, even if you tried) based on your electromagnetic signature: What is the signature composed of? What shapes your signal out into the Universe?

Dr. Dispenza says it like this, "The thoughts we think send an electromagnetic signal out into the field. The feelings we generate magnetically draw events back to us. Together, how we think and how we feel produces a state of being, which generates an electromagnetic signature that influences every atom in our world."

Each one of your thoughts — old conditioned thoughts that no longer serve you, just as well as empowering ones — create a frequency that influences your electromagnetic signature. Mixed together your signature is unique to you. Nobody else has this exact composition of thoughts and emotions. Thoughts do not stand alone. Every thought is followed by an emotion because as humans, we always look for meaning in what is happening "to" us.

A quick example: travel back to your high school years. Remember how in sports lessons we'd form teams and the captain would be able to choose his team members from the whole class? One person always got picked last. The thought is: "I got picked last to join the team." And immediately our brain searches for the meaning: "I must be the worst player in class. I'm not an asset, I only slow them down. Nobody likes me. I'm not good enough." The thought in itself is only a fact. Someone will always be the last one to get picked, no matter how good or bad a player they are. But the meaning we individually give the situation charges it with emotion.

Your thoughts aren't private. Your emotions aren't private. Your energy isn't private. You are part of the One Source. The Universe is always listening and responding.

The act of sending thoughts out into the energy field of the Universe is active. You think it, so you are active. The act of attracting it to you through emotion is a rather passive one. You are dwelling in a state of being and through being, you receive. It can be tempting to believe that we're not responsible for what shows up at our doorsteps, yet we always are.

"The state of your life is nothing more than a reflection of the state of your mind."
– Dr. Wayne Dyer

Make it work:

- What frequency of thought do you spend most of your day in? Positive or negative, loving or fearful? Give examples. Be honest. It's just us here.

- Take inventory: What is your current reality mostly composed of? Do good things happen? Or are you rather disappointed?

Mental Hygiene

How can you best control what you experience in life? The answer is simple, but mastery is challenging: control your thoughts and overall mindset.

Thoughts can either be high vibrational (in a loving, positive frequency) or low vibrational (fearful, negative frequency) — there is no gray area in between.

When you master your mindset, you can have anything you desire. That's why I've been putting so much emphasis on personal growth and self-awareness throughout this book. Often we say things in our mind that we would never say out loud — that doesn't mean it goes unnoticed. It becomes part of you. The more you repeat it and believe it, the more it becomes part of your overall energy signature. You're attracting into your life based on the frequency of the thoughts and attached emotions that you consistently emit into the field.

In my yoga teacher training, I learned a concept that struck me like lightning. Understanding the ancient yogic wisdom opened a door of empowerment for me. Consciousness is power. The more you understand how your energy field functions and what makes you tick, the easier and more fun it becomes to step into your power.

> *Thoughts determine your emotions.*
> *Your emotions determine your actions.*
> *Your actions determine your habits.*
> *Your habits determine your character.*
> *Your character determines your destiny.*
> *— from Sivananda Yoga Teacher Training*

Understanding this correlation was mind-blowing and a complete game changer for me. I loved it because it went past the mere thought and emotion aspect of cocreating your life. Your mindset determines your actions. Whatever you feed your mind, you ultimately start to believe and then you act accordingly. It suddenly made sense why affirmations work and why it's so important to keep a daily practice of mental hygiene.

Unfortunately, many still dismiss the importance of mindset. It is not so much about building another to-do in your already busy life. Changing your mindset to match the character of your best self doesn't have to be tedious. It can be a fun practice where you stay aware of *why* you respond, think, feel, and act a certain way. It is really not something you can do while sitting on your meditation pillow. You work on your mindset every minute of the day. You can only find the tricky disempowering beliefs that you carry by *living* your life. They will most easily reveal themselves in your everyday experiences. You don't have to travel the world, meditate in silent retreats, or sit at the feet of a guru (unless you want to).

You are your own guru. The truth and force of the universe is within you. Let me say it in the words of master Yoda from the movie *Star Wars*: "The force is strong with you."

Have you ever noticed that some movies speak to your soul? That movies, just like music, have the ability to bypass the restraints of logic and capture you in a truth that is only understood with your heart? Good movies speak to our emotions and hearts. They crack us open in ninety minutes, take us on a wild ride, and open our minds to new concepts. Some only understood with the heart. I'm always excited when I find a nugget of truth in movies.

"What is the most resilient parasite? An idea.
Resilient...highly contagious. Once an idea has taken hold of
the brain it's almost impossible to eradicate. An idea that is
fully formed — fully understood — that sticks;
right in there somewhere."
— Cobb, Leonardo DiCaprio's character in Inception

I know it can be daunting to fully allow new concepts to take hold of your mind. Your ego will try to talk you out of it. It will try to keep you going in the way you've always been going. It wasn't so bad after all.

But your heart knows. Your heart will vibrate in resonance with what you need right now on your path. Take what resonates and leave the rest. Other aspects may become relevant on another stretch of your journey and you can always return to this book to guide you into the expanse of your soul and Divine power.

The force (power of source) is strong within you, my dear. An idea planted in your mind can change your whole life. Be careful which ideas you allow to grow in your mind. Maybe it's time to weed out the negative mindset that's been keeping you stuck, small, detached from your true power and potential?

> *"As a single footstep will not make a path on the earth, so a*
> *single thought will not make a pathway in the mind.*
> *To make a deep physical path, we walk again and again.*
> *To make a deep mental path, we must think over and over*
> *the kind of thoughts we wish to dominate our lives."*
> *— Henry David Thoreau*

Make it work:

- How do you feel most of the time during the day? What's your predominant state of being?
- Which thoughts and emotions may be attracting the good or bad experiences into your life? Clarity is power! The more you know what is working and what's not, the easier you can shift to empowering thoughts and language.
- How are you talking to yourself every day? What are the phrases you repeat regularly? If you're not sure, it's time to notice! We are often incredibly hurtful toward ourselves.

"I say "Out" to every negative thought that comes to my mind. No person, place, or thing has any power over me, for I am the only thinker in my mind. I create my own reality and everyone in it."
— Louise Hay

Master Your Mindset

To attract what your heart and soul truly desire, you need to let go of all the disempowering beliefs that keep attracting experiences you do not desire. What's a good test to be sure you still have limiting mindset? Ask yourself if you have mastered all aspects of your life and living in full abundance and purpose.

My guess is, no. How do I know? If you were already resonating at the frequency of your purpose and soul desires, you'd have already manifested all of it. You'd be happily living your life and wouldn't be looking for answers.

For now (and always) awareness is power. The more aware you are of yourself, your beliefs, and motivation for action, the more in charge of your life you are. The more consciously and deliberately you are creating your reality.

When you start acting like a cocreator of your life, you realize you are in control of your thoughts, emotions, and focus. You decide what makes you smile. You decide what makes you happy. You decide what meaning you give a situation and with it, you control your reaction. You are fully in charge of your thoughts and emotions. Emotions are always a reaction to a thought. Start choosing better thoughts, trust them and believe in them, and watch your emotions change. Your whole state of being will change!

Remember that *who you are* is what counts, because your energy signature attracts from the field. Who you are is based on your state of being. Your state of being is controlled by your attention (focus), the meaning you give the situation (emotion), and posture (physiology).

"The primary cause of unhappiness is never the situation but your thoughts about it."
— Eckhart Tolle

The good news is that you are fully in control of all these influences on your state of being. You can steer your focus, give a positive meaning to a situation, and stand tall like the powerful cocreator that you are. Nobody can make you think or feel a certain way, unless you decide to believe their agenda and make it your own.

"It's not what you look at that matters, it's what you see."
— Henry David Thoreau

On this path of becoming a deliberate cocreator, you are responsible for your well-being. It's your responsibility to make empowering decisions that will lead you closer to living a life you love. The world will pull you, push you, and try to weave you back into its illusions. Your ego will try to make you believe that all this conscious creation stuff doesn't work. Let it try. It is *your* choice whether you believe it or not.

Remember, whatever you choose to believe in *will* come true because you draw it in through your energy. The good news: if you don't like what you have created this far, you can make a new choice every moment of your life. Every moment holds the power to reconnect you back to your elemental power of creation. Every moment, you can choose to become a new version of yourself.

> *"The moment you become aware of the ego in you, it is*
> *strictly speaking no longer the ego, but just an old,*
> *conditioned mind-pattern. Ego implies unawareness.*
> *Awareness and ego cannot coexist."*
> *– Eckhart Tolle*

Make it work:

- How can you control your daily focus? What you put into your mind will always have a reaction: conditioned and emotional. Can you clear out your Instagram feed to make it more positive, watch less news, be around uplifting people…find ways to make your life more positive.

- What do you choose to believe to be true about your life, purpose, and destiny? What energy signature would you like to have?

- Movie stars step into character when they star in a movie. They leave their personality at the door and impersonate someone new. Use your work from the chapters before where you rewrote your story and combine it with the insights you got here, to create an avatar of who you are as the best version of you. How does she dress? How does she speak? What's her posture? What's her character like? What does she believe to be true about the world? You're creating an alter ego that you can step into anytime you desire. Superman's alter ego is Clark Kent; Batman's alter ego is Bruce Wayne. Your alter ego is Super-You. Describe in detail your full potential on purpose living "Super-You." Be specific.

- Use your alter ego in everyday life. It's not enough to write this down. Dress like her, talk like her, be her!

Fast Lane to Energy Mastery

There is a fast route to bypass the ego and its acceptance of the concepts that we just discussed. It will put you into perfect harmony with the Universe so your desires can be sent out in crystal clarity and keep you open to receiving the blessings back into your life: Gratitude.

Through the practice of gratitude, you infuse your mind and energy field with positivity. You raise your vibration and frequency to attract back to you the positive experiences you desire for your life.

Gratitude for everything you already have signals to the Universe that you'd like more to be grateful for. The Universe knows what you think and if you were thinking, for instance, "I don't have enough money," this is exactly what you would experience. The Universe does not label a thought as good or bad. Whatever you say or think repeatedly will become part of your life. It sticks like glue. That's why we rewrote your story a few steps past. If you keep saying, thinking, and feeling the same way, you will keep attracting the resemblance of that in your life.

Begin by being grateful for everything you already have. Focus on what is going well to amplify this emotion. You are attracting from the field through your emotional blueprint. A grateful energy signature attracts more to be grateful for. Lack attracts more lack. Fear attracts more fear. Love attracts more love. The safest and fastest route to cocreating more of what you want is to acknowledge everything you already have that feeds this emotional signature.

Make it work:

- Make a list of everything that you're grateful for in your life. Start by choosing the area you'd most like to change. There's always something to be grateful for; be open to shifting your focus from victim to creator. Notice how it makes you feel to have all these good things in your life.

- Just FYI, I'll be sharing more about how to best use gratitude to create your best life in the next step.

- Create positive statements (affirmations) as a way to reprogram your mind toward what you desire. Whenever you move into a thought that doesn't serve your highest goals, change it into something positive. For instance, "I don't know how to find my purpose" can turn into "Every day, in every way, I am moving closer to living a life on purpose. I trust the process."

The How

Our world is linear. As humans, we think in terms of past, present, and future. We measure time in durations and we want to control what happens around us. That's why so many ask how can I get this, how can I find that, how will my desire come to me? We are trained to believe that we need to know the path and the exact steps on *how* to get from point A to B in our lives.

If you are ready to draw upon your true creator powers, then linear paths are obsolete. You are a multidimensional being outside of time and space having a human body and making a linear experience. It's part of the big game we signed up for and the one who transcends the rules of the game masters it.

What I'm saying is, you don't need to know *how* things, people, or experiences will come to you. That's the job of the Universe to deliver to you. Your job is to step into the frequency of what you desire so the Universe can deliver.

Read that again: Your job is to master your energy so that the frequency of the signal is aligned with your desires. This way, the Universe can do its job and bring you what you desire. The Universe takes care of *HOW* things will manifest in your life.

"Abundance is not something we acquire.
It is something we tune into."
– Wayne Dyer

First Signs of Progress

A few words on using your manifesting powers as a cocreator. As you get started, please keep in mind that you may first create experiences that seem like failure or blocks on your path. That's *NOT* what it is. For you to move ahead on your path of purpose, the Universe will first show you where you are *not yet* in alignment with your desires.

When you set an intention to manifest a desire, you will first attract experiences that show you in which ways you're not yet aligned with your goal. It's not a message to stop, but to eliminate the obstacles to reach your dreams.

It's *not* a sign that your manifestation doesn't work. Instead it is a sign of progress, because the universe has answered your intention. Your task then is to locate the beliefs, programs, and habits connected to what's showing up and release them.

The Universe's message to you in this case is:

"Great. I got your order and I want to deliver. But for me to be able to deliver, you need to adjust your energy signal. Currently, you are not a match to the experience you desire. I cannot yet bring it to you. Please let go of these beliefs, habits, and energies. If you do, your energy frequency will be aligned with your desire so you can receive."

This is important to know because so many people give up and think the law of attraction doesn't work for them. It works for others, but not for them. These people give up when just a tiny bit of headwind comes up. Don't buy into the chatter of the ego that you are not capable or worthy enough. Your mind chatter will try to tell you that it's too much work, too complicated, that it won't work. That's okay. Don't believe it. Breathe. Reconnect to your heart.

Your heart radiates a deep desire to expand into all that you are throughout every cell of your body at every moment in time.

Awareness is the ultimate key to letting go of limiting beliefs. If you are not aware of a destructive, disempowering, and limiting program running in your energy field, you can't stop it. That's why it is so essential for you to become very aware of your motives, drivers, and reasons for taking actions. Certain circumstances will trigger emotions within you that lead you to take action. Self-inquiry will give you the answers that will help you transform yourself into a conscious creator that walks boldly toward purpose. Living a life on purpose means stepping into your full potential and owning your place in this Universe as a cocreator.

> *"You leave old habits behind by starting out with the thought, 'I release the need for this in my life.' "*
> *— Dr. Wayne Dyer*

Summary Step #4:

- There is a quantum energy field (aka The Universe/Spirit/God or whatever you call it) that carries infinite potential and abundance.

- You are composed of 99.9 percent energy and 0.1 percent matter, which means you are part of this quantum energy field.

- You take an ongoing and active part in creation through the electromagnetic signature of your energy field.

- Your energy field is unique to you and it is shaped by your thoughts and emotions. You can also call this your state of being or "who you are."

- Your thoughts send out electromagnetic signals to the quantum field.

- Your emotions attract back experiences, things, and people from the quantum field into your field of experience, your reality.

- Positive thoughts and emotions have a higher frequency (pulse faster) and create faster manifestations, than lower vibrational (negative) thoughts.

- You can deliberately create from the quantum field by choosing thoughts and emotions that are aligned with your desires.

- You must be self-aware and keep a mental hygiene focused on what you want to create, to master the art of manifesting from thought form into physical form.

- It is not your job to control how things manifest into physical form. Your job is to master your own energy signal to attune it to your desires. You do this by mastering your mindset, emotions, and with it your overall state of being.

- You can change your state by changing your focus, by changing what meaning you give something, by changing your emotion about it, and by choosing a different posture or working on your physiology.

- A great way to step into a more powerful version of yourself is to create an alter ego and act as if until you have fully embraced *being* that better version of yourself.

- As a sign of progress, you may encounter blocks at first. This only means that the Universe is showing you what you need to let go of first, before you can receive what you desire.

Step #5

Take Inspired Action

"Stop acting so small.
You are the universe in ecstatic motion."
– Rumi

Let me guess what you're thinking, "All this sounds good, but what do I do?! I'm an action taker; I don't sit around and wait for stuff to magically appear."

I hear you. I'm the same way and between us, taking action is a crucial part of manifesting that many miss out on. *The Secret* books missed out on mentioning that sitting around speaking affirmations without taking inspired action will *not* make you rich. It's a big reason why the law of attraction gets such a bad rap these days.

Just to be clear, yes, action on your part is required to make your dream life a reality. And it's going to be action beyond your self-awareness and mindset work. The mindset work will shed the layers that keep distorting the guidance from your essence, but once you hear your guidance, you *will take inspired action based on the clear guidance* to cocreate with the Universe. *Cocreate.* The Universe will come fifty percent of the way, but you have to go the other fifty percent.

Changing the Right Way

Why is it so endlessly hard for us to take action outside our comfort zone? Change is hard for us humans! We love routines because they keep us safe and make our lives so much easier. Our brains love to store repetitive tasks on autopilot. Just remember when you learned how to drive a car. Wasn't it overwhelming to do everything at once — blink, push the brake, find the right gear, check the mirrors, steer the wheel, pay attention to traffic, and so on. But with time, driving a car became easier, didn't it? After a while, you do all these things simultaneously without *consciously* thinking about it. You've trained your brain and body memory to do all these things without the need of your full conscious orders. The brain loves sticking to what it knows because it saves energy and makes life so much easier.

When we look at it from a psychological point of view, we are designed to avoid pain to survive. Pain doesn't always mean that you're in a life or death situation. Pain can be anything from a difficult conversation, to exercise, or getting up from the couch on a rainy Sunday afternoon. We are constantly deciding what will give us pleasure or pain. Then we avoid the things that cause pain and increase the things that give us pleasure. That's how simple we humans operate. Pain and pleasure can be linked to anything. It's your unique conditioning and you can change it, once you become aware of it.

Here's an easy example. Jennifer starts a new diet every month, but she never sticks with it or loses the weight she wants to. She's trying to introduce positive change into her life to be more healthy and have more energy. Why does she fail to reach her goal? Logically it doesn't make sense because the pleasure of health should exceed the pleasure of eating unhealthy foods. Logically Jennifer agrees and despairs even more. She thinks she is not strong enough and something must be wrong with her because by now, she thinks she's the only undisciplined person in the whole world. When we look deeper at what drives Jennifer, we may find the answer. What is her pleasure and pain composition when it comes to dieting? Being overweight is painful. Being slim, healthy, and vibrant is pleasurable. Letting go of her evening feast that helps her unwind and relax: very painful. Going to the fitness studio to work out where everybody is fit instead of eating: very painful.

Do you see the big picture? Although Jennifer wants to lose weight and she thinks it will be pleasurable once she achieves it, she has little immediate motivation to change. Everything she needs to do *now* (skip her feast and feel ashamed working out) to reach pleasure inflicts tremendous pain on her. The pain is bigger than the pleasure. Well, how can she turn that around? She needs to link *immediate pain* to eating and not working out. She has been conditioned to link pleasure to food. But she can change her conditioning about food and change her life completely, by changing her pain/pleasure composition.

For a few years in college I smoked cigarettes. I wanted to stop; when I had a drink I'd always crave a cigarette with it. Talking about conditioning, huh? I wasn't a heavy drinker at all, but still it bothered me that I'd grab a smoke when I was out with friends. So, the pleasure of the experience exceeded the pain of the disgusting taste and headaches the next morning. How did I quit my undesired behavior? I imagined the smoke going down to my lungs and turning them dark from the tar. I totally immersed myself in that picture and experience until I found it way too disgusting to ever pick up a cigarette again. Every time I saw a cigarette that picture would pop up and keep me from smoking. The pain of feeling disgusted and having the tar flood my lungs exceeded the pain of not having a cigarette with my drink. Done deal.

I once heard a woman say she vowed she'd eat a can of dog food live on camera if she broke her diet. She made it through the diet! The pain of eating dog food and being humiliated in front of people was bigger than sticking to her outlined meals. Whatever works, right?

Change is not easy for anybody. Especially when we want to make big life changes, our human nature seems to conspire against us. You know now that your ego will try to talk you out of making a change, that your beliefs system needs an overhaul, and that your conditioning may make it even harder on you to create positive momentum. You are equipped with the tools to face the challenge and rise to the top of your game. You know how to deal with the obstacles that will show up along the way.

Make it work:

- Put it to the test right now. What have you been wanting to change, but never succeeded? What causes you pain in the situation? In which way does the pain outweigh the pleasure? How can you connect immense pain to *NOT* changing?

- What pain/pleasure do you currently link to following your purpose?

- How can you link pain to *not following* your purpose? Or the other way around — how can you link tremendous pain to continue living life without purpose?

- How can you link tremendous *pleasure* to following your purpose?

"Personal power is directly tied to personal responsibility, which most people avoid."
— *Brendon Burchard*

Aligned Action

Now that you're ready to take action, you may be wondering what actions are the right ones. You're ready to ditch the nine to five and get off the hamster wheel. You're motivated and excited to create a life you love living intentionally and purposefully.

But how do you know which actions will take you there and which ones won't? It's not about massive action in the wrong direction. We're done with that.

If you've worked through the exercises in this book, by now you have a good idea of what your dream life looks like, what your talents and gifts are, and in which way they can contribute to all of life. But you're still looking for the plan that will take you from place A to place B.

I have good and bad news for you. Let's start with the bad news, shall we?

The bad news: There is no linear plan.

I know you'd love a step-by-step plan to follow to reach your purpose. You'd feel safe, in control, equipped, and confident. Sorry, it doesn't work that way. There are two reasons for that:

#1 – Free Will: You have free will choices, so you decide at every moment in time how and what happens *for* you. You can make detours, go fast or slow, but there is not one linear plan that is laid out for you. That's also why you were able to move in a direction that you now realize is not to your highest good.

#2 – Potential: Your soul has a potential that it can live up to in this life. By living your full potential you could, for instance, become the president of the United States, or you could become a different type of influential leader. There is not *one* end goal and you won't be awarded a trophy. Your destination is who you become in the process. When you're walking your path to more purpose, you draw upon infinite potentials from the universal field that you can use *for* you. You are not limited to one path. But the path that will be most fulfilling is the one that you feel is right for you and that you actively choose.

The good news: You have all wisdom within you already.

#1 – Cocreation: Don't forget that your energy, thoughts, and emotions *create* your world. You are fully in charge of what comes to you. That's great news, because it means you make your own destiny. Sure, there are different potentials for you to fulfill, but in the end, it's your choice which one you'll act upon. You are part of the Universe and you interact with it in every moment of time.

#2 – Intuition: Listen up, this one's important. By attuning yourself to Spirit (to your soul essence and source), you supercharge your intuition. Spirit guides you through conceptual, intuitive messages. Spirit doesn't give you an outline on what to do next. Your next steps could change the moment you set a new intention or make a new choice. To create your most amazing life, you need to create a relationship with Spirit, your source, God, or whatever you like to call your creator. Spirit guides you through your intuitive feelings. You are one; all knowledge is accessible within you at all times.

I can't emphasize enough how important it is for you to attune your energy field to source energy. The more you are in harmony with your soul essence, the easier decisions will be, and the faster you'll move ahead on your path. The Universe is eager to help and support you with any of your desires because you *are* the Universe. It's basically helping itself. I understand that this is a new way of making decisions for you and it can feel daunting to hand your decisions over to an infinite intelligence that you can't understand logically. The wisdom of your heart is powerful though. Through your heart you get the raw, true messages that aren't tainted by ego or fear.

I stood where you are right now. I didn't know how to listen to my heart or even to distinguish my head from my heart guidance. It was all a big blur. I knew that all my power lies in the clarity of my connection to my soul and source energy, but I was unsure how to strengthen it.

Yet, I didn't give up and devoted time every single day to connect with spirit, angels, and my spirit guides. I kept finding ways to silence the ego and chip away at clearing old mindset and blocks from my energy field. It has made all the difference to my life, happiness, and fulfillment. Through this practice, I opened up my psychic senses, I became a powerful healer, and have deep, meaningful (and really entertaining) conversations with Gods, Angels, Goddesses, Ascended Masters, and so forth.

There are things in this world that can be understood with the mind and that's great. I'm not some delusional hippie who lives on the outskirts of civilization, as you know by now. But I also know that life is magical. And by believing in miracles, you open yourself up to receiving them. The Universe wants to live more through you. It wants you to be more, do more, and have more. All the abundance can come to you if you don't stop it with your own thoughts of limitation, lack, and control.

In the next chapter, I'll share with you how you can create your own relationship with your source/soul/Spirit so you can get clear guidance and healing and cocreate your purposeful life much faster.

Make it work:

- What is your vision of your best life?
- How are you contributing to this vision every day (even if it's just baby steps for now)?

- Where will you end up, if you don't consciously decide on a destination for your life?

- Where are you heading right now? List all positive and negative outcomes.

- Try to make it a habit to check in with your intuition on how each decision and action makes you feel. Are you moving closer or further away from your life purpose?

- *High impact question alert*: What's the *gain* of not taking action? In which way are you benefitting? It may be that you don't have to face your fears, get uncomfortable, or have an honest discussion. Once you shed light on how you're cheating your progress by experiencing short-term pleasure, you can transcend the situation and get moving.

Summary Step #5:

- The mindset and self-awareness work sheds the layers that keep distorting the guidance from your essence.

- Once you hear your guidance loud and clear, you need to take inspired action to cocreate with the Universe.

- You cocreate with the Universe: The Universe will come fifty percent of the way, but you have to go the other fifty percent.

- Human behavior is steered by pain and pleasure. We operate on autopilot to increase pleasure and avoid pain. Knowing this will help you to identify your own conditioning and make it easier to create lasting change.

- Your ego will try to talk you out of making a change, your beliefs systems need an overhaul, and your pain/pleasure conditioning may make it even harder on you to create positive momentum — but you have the tools now.
- Knowledge is the seed of action. Knowledge without action is worth absolutely nothing, so never leave the site of a decision without taking immediate action.
- Living from your essence means taking *inspired, intentional action* over massive action.
- There is no linear action plan available that will lead you to purpose.
- But you have all the knowledge within you already and you access its intuitive, conceptual by bringing yourself into harmonic frequency with your soul (source energy or Spirit)
- The more you are in harmony with source energy, the easier decisions will be, and the faster you'll move ahead on your purposeful path.
- The Universe is eager to help and support you with any of your desires because you *are* the Universe. It's basically helping itself.
- This is a new way of making decisions for you and it can feel daunting to hand your decisions over to an infinite intelligence that you can't logically understand. The wisdom of your heart is powerful though. Through your heart, you get the raw, true messages that aren't tainted by ego or fear.

- The Universe wants to live more through you. It wants you to be more, do more, and have more. All the abundance can come to you if you don't stop it with your own thoughts of limitation, lack, and control.

Step #6

Attune to Your Soul Essence

"Everything in the universe is within you.
Ask all from yourself."
– Rumi

When you're attuned to Spirit, the Infinite Intelligence of the Universe, you receive accurate guidance. You can use the wisdom of the Universe to help you find the best possible outcomes for you and anybody involved. You can ask this intelligence to show you the steps, path, or decisions that are to your highest good. No more relying on your own limited frame of reference in your logical mind that is often infused with the fears of the ego. Complete game changer!

Since you are part of the Universe, your creator knows you. The Supreme knows your mind, hears your intentions, worries, and concerns. It always wants the best for you and supports you endlessly in magical ways.

You don't even need to be clear about what you ask of it. You could also just say, "Dear Spirit, this is what I want, I just don't know how to get there."

But what type of answer and guidance are you looking for? Probably the heavens won't part and an Angel won't descend from heaven with a roadmap to get to where you want to go. What you will receive though, is *intuition in you on how to do it.*

The answers are inside of you. Spirit will speak through you, move through you, guide you to see, hear, feel, and know what you need to get to your desired destination. If you are confused on how to find your purpose, what timing is right, and what your next steps are, all you need to do is express it to your ever-benevolent creator. The Universe loves you, stands by you, and will always answer your call. But you have to ask for its help or it will respect your free will choice of doing it all by yourself.

What's so difficult to grasp is that as humans, we are asking in a linear way. But the Universe doesn't give linear answers. The Universe is not linear. We are only having a linear experience here on earth, yet in truth, we are also multidimensional beings. Time does not exist. So, infinite intelligence, well aware of different dimensions and realities, will answer in an intuitive, conceptual way. It gives you signs, opportunities, messages of potential that you can choose to use or dismiss.

Source Energy

When we try to understand source energy, we are really trying to understand who we are. Our quest of ever searching for more — to have more, do more, and be more — is the expression of the Divine working through us. Our Divine source is the power that pulls us forward and lets us spin in a restless whirl of ambitions, dreams, and desires. Our aspirations are a sign of the Divine pulsing through our veins and energy field. Every aspect of who we are is Divine perfection. And there is a part within us that longs to comply and reunite with source. Our soul knows who we are. It has been there through the centuries, the lifetimes, the higher dimensions, and keeps storing all this wisdom for us. We are not only human, we are a soul as well. Just because we're having a human experience, it doesn't mean all the higher knowledge is gone. It only means that it's in storage so that we can fully be present in the human experience we're having right now.

Yet the energy and essence of source, of unconditional love, is always within us if we choose to attune ourselves to it. Have you ever met a person who's had that "je ne sais quoi?" These people have a pull; we are drawn to them although we often don't really know why. It's that they are living in their essence, they are shining their Divine light strongly. They are attuned to source and strongly radiate source energy. Aren't we fascinated by them? The truth is, we are fascinated by their Divine spark, we see our own light, our own essence, reflected back to us. The brilliance, radiance, and light they emulate is the brilliance and light that lives within each one of us. It is the source of our being.

It is the power of our true (Divine) self that we can feel responding in the cells of our body. Being in the presence of a being that is attuned to source power is magical. It opens the door for us to see and feel our own divinity, brilliance, and power. Source energy is full potential, it is ever growing, always becoming. It is strong in those people who are growing into more of who they are, because life (source) always looks to express itself more fully. When a seed is planted in the earth and with it given a chance to thrive, it immediately starts bursting into more life and a fuller expression of its being. A seed doesn't stay a seed. A flower never stays closed if it is ready to bloom. Nature doesn't block life from pulsing, expressing, and living through it. What about us humans? Don't we often block life's fullest expression through us because we're afraid, worried, full of doubt and uncertainty of what might happen?

Make it work:

- Did you ever shy away from being all that you can be, from outshining others or maybe being afraid of whether you can or can't do it? Trust the first thoughts and ideas that come to you. What happened in those moments? Why did you shy away from progress?
- Note down the mindset patterns that are ready to be released. Turn the statements around into positive affirmations.

Maybe you're thinking that this sounds nice, but it's too fluffy. Well, I'm sure some conscious or unconscious part of you has a deep desire to reattune to source. It shows up in the search for meaning in life and a search for deep love. Many people travel the world and are searching on the outside for a thing, experience, or person to fill this void. While we can satisfy our desires on the outside for some time, it never lasts. It's like a patch we press on the wound and after a while it falls off, leaving us even more desperately aching for more. Our collective wound is the illusion of separation from our creator. In truth we are not separated, because we have the ability to tune into source energy, use it, and create from it every second of every day. Many people on this planet just aren't initiated or interested in these spiritual gems of knowledge.

When you are attuned to source, you are aligned to receive clear guidance for your life. Don't we all struggle with decisions because we're afraid to make a wrong one? When you tune into your soul essence and are in harmony with the Supreme, you are tapped into your superpowers. The spiritual senses that we are born with, but only few of us train. Growing up, we learn to distrust our intuition and psychic senses. The less we train our intuition muscle, the more we lose our gift of inner knowing. But it's never too late to reconnect to your essence. The advantages are manifold. You'll know things without having an explanation for it, you can read people's energies and motives. You'll be able to see visions and get answers from Spirit much faster and clearer than ever before. Your spidey senses will peak and you'll feel like your intuition is on fire.

Your Spidey Senses

Sometimes it seems so mystical how people tune into source and heal or give Divine guidance. It's funny because in the end, it's really our most natural state to be in flow and harmony with all that is. In past centuries, only the most initiated and prepared were taught how to consciously receive Divine guidance and work with its potent energies. The overall frequencies of the planet were much lower, so there had to be a lot of preparation to be able to tune in. Rituals were a major part of raising the vibration so the higher frequencies could be accessed. We're in a special time now, because the energy of our planet is rapidly ascending to higher frequencies.

This makes it easier for us to awaken to our soul essence and receive spiritual knowledge.

What I've found on my spiritual journey is that being tuned in is our most natural state of being. Nothing needs to be added to tap into source; it's rather a dropping of all unnecessary concepts. Essentially, it's doing less instead of doing more. Counterintuitive concept when we're trained to believe that doing more will bring achievement and success. I know for me it was really hard to just be. Being with yourself can be one of the most challenging and transformational encounters you ever have.

Most of the time we're cutting ourselves off by believing in our stories and the illusion of separation. But as you know by now, there is no separation. We are all connected through eternity. Unless we are fully self-realized, we are always bouncing back and forth between belief systems, fears, love, desire, and any other emotional or mental construct. Our mind is constantly focusing on something, interpreting situations, and reacting through emotion or physical action. It keeps us busy trying to make sense of this world and our place in it.

Our mind can take us anywhere and it usually does! If we are not in control of our mind, it will take over and create uncensored concepts of fear and drama. The mind will automatically go to negativity if we do not actively train it to interpret things in a more constructive way. The mind's job is to keep up the illusion of separation and to keep us from harm so that we can survive in our physical bodies. If left undirected, our mind will always go to this default setting and look for harm, drama, trauma, and fear. It is fearful by nature because it constantly lives with the threat that you may realize it's not real and make it obsolete. The ego mind will do anything to keep you believing its stories. I'm figuring one of the people who most struggle with happiness must be lawyers. All day long, they are training their mind to "look for the catch." Then they go home to their family and their mind doesn't stop functioning that way when they enter the door. It keeps looking for the catch, so it may become increasingly difficult to trust and create deep intimacy.

Or think of mothers — they want to protect their child from harm no matter what. So, whatever the child does, the mother looks at with the eyes of, "What could go wrong here?" or "What dangers are lurking?" She is basically always looking at any negative scenario that may happen to be prepared to take immediate action to save her child from harm. While that is completely normal and an expression of love, mothers just don't change as the child grows up. You can be thirty-five years old, going on a vacation in India, and your mother will be worried something may happen. It gets intensified if they are not around to prevent it, doesn't it?

Okay, now that we know what is constantly tugging at our attention, let's dive into how you can tune in and maybe even stay tuned into spirit.

"Truly I tell you, unless you change and become like little children, you will never enter the kingdom of heaven."
— Jesus, Bible Matthew 18:3

In which way are little kids different from adults? What are the first characteristics that pop into your mind? Is it maybe that little kids are fearless, trusting, happy for no reason, always in the present moment, authentic, loving, caring, curious, interested, always amazed by new discoveries and the wonders of life? Little kids are definitely in the flow — they don't resent yesterday and they don't worry about tomorrow. They are always in the present moment because they don't even understand the concept of time. At some age, they start understanding past, present, and future, but length of time and precise timing is difficult to grasp for them. Hasn't everybody had the pleasure of traveling with a child and have it asking every two minutes when you'll finally arrive? Your answer means nothing to them; all they know is it's not *now*.

What children naturally know how to do is to be in the present moment with an open heart without worries and in complete faith. That's what the bible quote is about. It doesn't mean deteriorating in intellect or any other strange idea. For adults either of these two — an open heart or being fully present — have become a major challenge. I want you to be able to notice how it feels different to be tuned in vs. tuned out.

Connecting to your source, to spirit, is really simple. There is no complicated voodoo formula or crazy ritual you have to orchestrate. Instead, all you need is to be present in the energy of love. Be fully present in the moment with an open heart. This is your most potent state of being. You can get into this state by practicing gratitude.

Too many people live their complete life tuned out and cut off from source and wonder why they don't have any sense of fulfillment or happiness. Others naturally vibe in a state of flow because they appreciate life. They aren't scared to follow their desires and increase their own life by letting source energy express itself through them.

Let me show you how you can deliberately cultivate a strong connection to the very source of who you are so you can use these spiritual and metaphysical energies to strengthen your personal power.

Before I tell you exactly how to plug into source energy and realign with your soul's essence, a fair word of warning. I've said it before — this work transforms you. Once you open up your consciousness to a new world view, you won't be the same again. It's a bit like opening Pandora's Box (in a good way though). What you unleash will become a part of you and alter your state of being, seeing, and experiencing life. You will become more sensitive to harsh energies and may even find that people, places, and experiences that you once enjoyed won't bring you joy anymore. No need for fear, because obviously you've been guided here. Still, you have free will choices, so I feel obliged to tell you what you're getting yourself into (still in a good way.) So, please check your intentions for moving ahead in this book. Are you 100 percent committed to learning, integrating, and living the spiritual principles you'll expose yourself to in the most graceful and easy way? If you set this intention now, you'll have much more support.

Are you ready to soar?
The more grounded you are, the higher you fly.

Your Ten Tools to Attune to Source Energy

I'll share ten of my best tools to help you reconnect to your soul essence. The way to use them is to create your own routine and not overwhelm yourself with too many all at once. Try to start off with one or two and commit to do them for a week. If that goes well, add onto them. If it doesn't go so well, try another one and see if that's what you need at this point in time. I've created a calendar for you in your free workbook that you can download here: sharonkirstin.com/bookbonus

Look at the "frequency" I assigned to each tool to help you navigate which ones to practice daily, weekly, or as you wish. The more you practice these tools to consciously tune into your essence (who you really are on a soul level), the more you will vibrate at an energy frequency that matches source consciousness. Plain speaking, the more powerful, clear, and energized you will be to create your life of purpose.

Tool #1

Grounding

Security and Healing

Level of difficulty: Beginner

Time effort: Little

Frequency: Daily

Benefits: Increases sense of security in a stressful world, increases ability to retain information (great before studying), increases presence, connects to the healing core of the earth for releasing lower energies in the chakras, body and energy field, increases your vibration by drawing up the healing light-filled energies of the earth

Myth: It connects you to the drama of the world.

Goal: Stay connected to the nourishing energy of Mother Earth to boost your spiritual and personal progress.

Maybe you've heard of a grounding practice before. It means you anchor your energy in planet earth. For a long time, I felt resistance to grounding myself energetically. I didn't quite understand what it was good for and I thought it would "bring me down." That wasn't what I wanted. My desire was to connect to the Universe, to spirit, to higher wisdom. I wanted to feel the bliss of this beautiful, light and free energy that I felt during meditation. To be quite frank, some part of me just didn't want to be here and at that time, it felt like a downer to root myself into the planet.

The more sensitive I became the harsher and more uncomfortable I felt the energies around me and I really didn't want any part of it. I thought when I grounded myself, I would tune into the drama, pain, and lower energies that are still present on earth. Maybe you have a similar association with grounding? All I can say — don't stumble over the same limiting belief as me. Maybe you are indifferent and think it's just not necessary because you've been feeling fine all along (who knows how much better you could feel...). Either way you're in for a big delicious treat! Mother Earth is not the drama that is happening on her. Mother Earth is a powerful light being of her own with beautiful, powerful, transformational energy. What a breakthrough I had when I finally connected myself to the most pristine light in the *core* of the earth.

Visit www.sharonkirstin.com/bookbonus to get access to your workbook with an exclusive daily spiritual practice planner.

Grounding Practice:

Sit down on a chair with your feet flat on the ground, your back straight, and the palms of your hands facing upward resting in your upper thighs. Slightly tuck in your chin so that your neck lengthens. Breathe deeply. Take deep breaths in all the way down into your belly and exhale completely emptying your lungs. Breathe through your nose and put your attention on your body and breath.

When you feel present in the moment, set the intention to let roots grow from the soles of your feet and/or your tailbone all the way down into the core of the earth. It is very important that your intention is to lock into the core of the planet and not ground yourself superficially like a tree. In your mind's eye, visualize the most pristine light at the center of the earth and see your roots connecting in.

When you see or feel that you are connected, begin using your breath to draw the pristine light up into your body. Inhale and see the light streaming up into your body. On the exhale, release energies that no longer serve you for transmutation down into the core. You don't have to worry that your lower energies clog or strain earth. In her light, no negativity can prevail and she effortlessly dissolves any lower energies.

You can sit and feel her light move through your body and notice the affects you feel on your energy and well-being, or you can consciously direct the light through your chakras to strengthen, clear, and heal them. If you choose to move through your chakras, I suggest you use your breath. With the next inhale, visualize earth's light gathering in your root chakra, clearing, energizing, and strengthening it. Exhale and let it go. With your next breath, draw the light further up into your sacral chakra. Hold it there until you feel it is done and let it go on the exhale. Continue through all your chakras and notice how your whole energy field changes.

Set the intention to stay grounded throughout the whole day. Notice how different you feel throughout the day. Notice your energy levels and happiness. Check in sporadically if you are still well grounded, and if the connection feels weak, visualize that you are connecting back in. Use your breath again. This doesn't have to take long and you can do it at any point during the day in a few seconds. The more you practice, the stronger and faster you can establish your connection, and at some point, you will continuously hold it.

Tip: If you are having a hard time connecting to the core as described above, you can also visualize that you are moving down into the core of the earth. See yourself sliding down and immersing yourself in the light. Inhale it in through the pores of your body into your whole being. For beginners, this is often the easiest way to start and feel the connection.

Tool #2

Meditation

Guidance and Healing

Level of difficulty: Beginner

Time effort: Little

Frequency: Daily

Effects: Centering, decreases brain fog, decreases stress, increases peacefulness, increases calm, rejuvenates, increases immune system, decreases inflammation in the cells, decreases pain, decreases depression, increases positive emotions, decreases feelings of loneliness, increases empathy, helps regulate your emotions, increases self-control, increases gray brain matter, increases focus and productivity, increases creativity, improves memory

Myths: You need to have an empty mind. You need to sit for a long time. There are rules you need to follow.

Goal: Train yourself to detach from the ego and start noticing that your thoughts are *not* your identity. Become mindful of your energy and body. Actively draw high-vibrational source energy into your energy field. Become one with all that is in the present moment. Access higher spiritual knowledge. You can also set a specific intention for each meditation.

There are countless ways to meditate — mantra meditation, mindfulness meditation, guided meditations (I love these! I channel them and offer them on my website sharonkirstin.com, if you want to check them out), transcendental meditation, Yoga Meditations, Loving Kindness Meditation, Vipassana Meditation, and the list goes on. It may sound challenging to find the right meditation for you from the sea of practices. I won't be writing an essay here on each of these practices.

Instead I want to show you a simple and easy way to use meditation in a way that is authentic to you. If you feel drawn to investigate one of the mentioned meditation styles further, then feel free to do so. But for now, let me share my meditation best practices with you. Another word: just because you've tried meditation before and it "didn't work" for you — don't disregard it right away. Successful people never say, "I tried this, it doesn't work" (especially when so much research proves incredible positive effects). They say, "Ok, what can I change to make it work for me." That could be anything from mindset (what are your beliefs about meditation), motivation, structure, environment, or adding enjoyable elements.

"The past gives you an identity and the future holds the
promise of salvation, of fulfillment in whatever form.
Both are illusions."
– Eckhart Tolle

The Now

Did you ever notice that your focus usually jumps from present to future to past, constantly interpreting, drawing references, and reacting? One of the most spiritual practices you can engage in is to draw your attention to the now-moment. You have probably heard this before, but I'd love for you to take a moment and soak in the information I'll give you. Often the problem is not that we don't know what to do, but that we simply don't do it! And then we keep going around looking for solutions that are more complex just to avoid putting the knowledge into practice and keeping busy so that we don't have to face ourselves.

This very moment in which you are reading this book is the most potent time in your life. And now, and now, and now. Every now-moment holds the potential for growth, healing, achievement, love, for everything really. Your past has no power and your future doesn't have power either. The past is gone and can't be changed. The future is not here yet, so you can't act in it. All you will ever have in your life is now-moment after now-moment. Now is the only time you are alive and able to act.

"All negativity is caused by an accumulation of psychological time and denial of the present. Unease, anxiety, tension, stress, worry — all forms of fear — are caused by too much future, and not enough presence. Guilt, regret, resentment, grievances, sadness, bitterness, and all forms of nonforgiveness are caused by too much past, and not enough presence."
– Eckhart Tolle

Meditation can give you access to the fullness of the now-moment. Clearing your mind and just being, instead of doing and thinking, lets you enter the world of being versus the constant doing. In the now you can enter into your soul expanse and become one with all that is. You access the knowledge of the all-mind and actively fuel yourself with high vibing energy that can cleanse your energy field.

There are two commonly used points that you can focus on to gather your energy and draw your attention inward. The third eye is located between and slightly above your eyebrows. It is your center and chakra of spiritual sight. When you strengthen, cleanse, and train your third eye, it usually becomes easier to receive visions and visual guidance. I used to meditate by focusing on my third eye in the beginning of my journey, but during my journey I realized that there's one spot in your body that is even more powerful. It's the other focus point I recommend: your heart center, also called your heart or heart chakra. When you can open your heart, you melt into one with source.

"Meditation is the only intentional, systematic human activity which at bottom is about not trying to improve yourself or get anywhere else, but simply to realize where you already are."
– Jon Kabat-Zinn

Mindfulness

Google defines mindfulness as "a mental state achieved by focusing one's awareness on the present moment, while calmly acknowledging and accepting one's feelings, thoughts, and bodily sensations." It is the practice of being in the moment with a complete focus on the present in full acceptance. How much time do you spend in the present moment aware of your body, emotions and thoughts? In our fast paced society it becomes a challenge to be present and in full contact with yourself.

I remember back when I had my role as a Director for an Online Fashion company, I wasn't aware of my body almost the whole day. Often I wouldn't even recognize a feeling of hunger unless a colleague asked me to go to lunch. I had to consciously stop and tune in to see whether I was hungry. Most of the time it was really more a routine than knowing that I needed food at that moment. Hunger is just a small example, although very relevant with so many of us eating out of emotional reasons rather than hunger.

Why is mindfulness important? We've learned before that our mind is constantly working — every moment of the day our brain is interpreting signals. It focuses (past, present, future), interprets what the meaning is of what it perceives (internal or external) based on past references (belief systems), and then it takes action. The actions can be external or internal or both. An emotion is just as much an action as is a decision followed by external action. Your state of being changes constantly based on what you make of a certain situation. What you believe about it will have an emotional reaction and this emotion will lead you to take action to either amplify it or stop it depending on whether it is a good or bad sensation for you. It is really a tug-of-war where we are constantly being drawn from the past to the future without an end. Our subconscious is constantly drawing on references from the past to make decisions and with that knowledge, it projects into the future deciding what to do in the present moment.

Mindfulness means paying attention in a particular way, on purpose, in the present moment nonjudgmentally.
— Jon Kabat-Zinn

The nonjudgment aspect of mindfulness is the key to enjoying the present moment. If you can train yourself to stop projecting into the future based on past references, you will find that right now. In the present moment you are fine. This is the moment where you can access happiness.

When you realize that unconditional happiness, love, and peace are available in this moment, you can shift the trajectory of your life. You will still have ambitions and strive for your dreams, but you won't give them the false expectation that acquiring something or being someone with a certain title will make you happy. Happiness is a decision. Happiness is not an achievement. Happiness comes from your reactions that are based on the meaning you give each thing that enters your life. This is why the worn-out saying — Life is one percent what happens to you and ninety-nine percent how you react to it — is actually true.

"There is no way to happiness. Happiness is the way."
—Thich Nhat Hanh

Breath or Pranayama

Notice right now how deeply you are breathing. Are you breathing shallow, short breaths or are you drawing air into your lungs deeply? It is an epidemic how few people really use their breath to draw in oxygen into their body. I mean, you know you need oxygen to live, but at the same time, you're never in the moment to notice your breath. Usually we are so busy we are not noticing our body. Yogis have made breath an integral part of their practice. They have a word for breath work: it's called pranayama. Prana means life force and yama as much as control. Pranayama is the art of controlling the life force. Yogis believe that air has prana in it and through absorbing it into your body, you recharge your own life force. Yogis use the breath to calm their mind but also to wake up their body. Breath can create a variety of experiences for you when you use it consciously.

I'd like to show you how you can use breath as the vehicle to full awareness of the present moment. It's easy actually; all you need to do is to consciously direct your attention to your breath. When you do this you are returning to the present moment. You can't focus on your breath and at the same time focus on the past or the future. This is your fast track to return to the here and now where all your power lies.

Easy does it – DIY your meditation practice:

Choose your location:

Ideally you should always meditate in the same location. If you do this often enough, you train your body and mind to go into a meditative state by itself. You condition yourself to enter a certain state. It's the same principle as going to bed. In your mind "bed" is connected to "sleeping." So, if you always go to sleep when you cuddle under the covers and close your eyes, this is what you're conditioning your body to do automatically. People who have trouble sleeping often (not always, again not doing a scientific research on sleep here) do other things in bed so that their brain is not singularly conditioned to rapidly go to sleep. The worst things you can do in bed is work — just FYI.

But you get the point: choose one place in your home as your meditation place. Every time you meditate you will sit in that space.

Choose a time:

Yoga tradition says the best time to meditate is in the morning between 4-6 am because the atmosphere is highly charged with spiritual power. I'm not going to make you get up at 4 am; don't worry. I want you to pick a time that works for you *every* day. Maybe you get up a bit earlier or maybe you take time before going to bed. You decide, but what you need to do is make a choice right now and schedule it in your calendar.

Choose a duration:

When you're just starting out you may not want to put a whole hour on the clock. Ten minutes is a great starting point and will already provide you with all the benefits mentioned before. You can also do ten minutes in the morning and ten minutes in the evening.

Choose your seat:

You can sit on the floor, on a meditation pillow, or on a chair. The only prerequisite is that it is not comfortable or you'll fall asleep. On a chair you won't lean your back against it. There are also meditation stools available that give comfort to your knees if that sounds like the right path for you. Depending on your choice of seat, you'll sit cross-legged (meditation pillow), or place your feet uncrossed next to each other flat on the floor (chair). Word of advice for the meditation pillow that I learned in my yoga teacher training: make sure your knees touch the floor. You need to choose a pillow that has enough padding so that while your legs are crossed your knees touch the floor. This is the most beneficial and enjoyable knee posture to avoid short-term pain and long-term strain. If your legs fall asleep don't worry about it in that moment.

Choose your mudra: (optional)

Mudra is the Sanskrit word for symbolic hand gestures. During meditation or pranayama (breath work), they direct the energy to certain parts of the body and stimulate the mind a certain way. In western countries, we also have a few of our own "mudras" like a thumb's up or a peace symbol. Just like ours, the Hindu mudras also have meanings. To keep this simple, here are your two choices:

No Mudra: Simply place your hands relaxed on your thighs palms facing upward (my favorite, talking about simplifying).

Gyan Mudra: The tips of the thumb and index finger touch lightly, while the rest of the fingers are gently stretched out. The hand is also placed relaxed on your thighs. This mudra is known as the "Seal of Knowledge" and helps unite the mind of the individual with the universal consciousness to access universal wisdom.

Choose your tunes: (optional)

You really don't need music or mantras to make your meditation practice powerful. I'll share two really good ones with you so that you can use them if it feels right. Experiment and see what works for you. A mantra is a Sanskrit word that symbolizes a sacred aspect of the Divine or even an incantation of the help and support of a God(dess).

OM: A spiritual sound said to encompass all words and with it all of life. In Sanskrit it is pronounced AUM. The meaning is threefold: A representing the awake state, U representing the dream state, and M representing the state of deep sleep. You'll find beautiful music where monks chant the sound OM on Spotify or probably even YouTube. It can support the depth of your meditation practice and let you enter into a deeper meditative state.

SOHAM: Again a Sanskrit word that means "I AM, the I AM." It is a mantra that reminds you that you are part of all that is. The "I AM" is source, God, all of creation. You are part of creation and this mantra helps you attune back to this truth.

Brainwave Entrainment: I use theta or alpha brainwaves in all the meditations I create for my audience. They aid to enter a deep state of relaxation because the waves slow down your brainwaves so you can access a meditative state much faster and more easily.

Set an intention:

Would you like to receive clarity, answers, enter a state of peace? What would you like this meditation to be about? Would you like to receive a healing? Raise your vibration? What's the outcome you'd like to receive? Set an intention before you start to get what you desire. The Universe loves clear requests.

Choose your focus point:

Third eye: Great spot to focus your attention when you're meditating on higher spiritual wisdom.

Heart center: My favorite — the heart center is the gateway to universal consciousness and becoming one with all that is. When you move into your heart center by thinking of something that makes you smile, you can feel instant expansion of your energy.

Breath: Concentrating on your breath will help you stay present in the moment. You can combine focus points by, for instance, concentrating on your third eye and breath at the same time. This helped me in the beginning because I was already busy keeping the focus and wasn't able to think too many other thoughts.

Mantra: Your mantra can serve as a focus that you return to and that keeps your mind from wandering.

During meditation:

Thoughts: Let all your thoughts come and go. Let them float by like leaves floating on a river. Don't attach to any of them. Your "monkey mind" will go crazy on you. That is to be expected. It does for all of us. It is a big misconception that in meditation you have no thoughts. In reality, you just don't attach to them. But you and I, we're human, so we *will* attach and follow a thought. No need to panic. As soon as you realize that you've attached to a thought, let it go in that moment and return to your focus point(s). Really often meditation is just this practice.

Tip: If you find yourself thinking about all the things you need to get done. Make a to-do list before sitting down in meditation so that you won't feel like you're forgetting something important.

Posture: The goal is to sit with a straight spine and not move throughout the time of the meditation. It is okay to readjust your spine posture when you find yourself crouching over, but make it a practice to stay as physically still as you can. A still body supports a quiet mind.

Meditation #1: Heart Center

Think of a cute baby animal or find a picture online (or check my Instagram for photos of my cute Chihuahua, Mojo). Notice what happens in your heart when you see the baby animal. We have a primal instinct to find them adorable and want to protect them. There must be a reason why cat videos are so popular. These videos have exactly this heart-opening effect on the viewers. We crave this feeling because intuitively we recognize it as our true nature. If you're not a big animal lover, then you can simply think of something — an experience or memory — that makes you smile.

Again, notice what happens in your heart center. You may feel your heart open, beat faster, or skip a beat. Usually it is best not to think of a particular person because we hold positive and negative emotions about people. It's not untainted so to say, and subconsciously, you are aware of all memories even though you may try to access a positive one. If you have a pet, I think you'll find it very easy. For me personally, I just need to think of my dog Mojo and how cute he moves when he is happy; that just does it for me every single time. I instantly drop into my heart center and a wave of connection and with it, love comes over me.

Experiment. Try it out and find your own way. The more you repeat the thought following by noticing your heart open, the more you are conditioning yourself, you are combining the two as cause and effect. This way with repetition, it becomes an automated response for your body to feel this way. You can trigger it in a moment and instantaneously swoop back into your heart center and with it into the present moment.

Meditation #2: Breath/Pranayama

Sit up straight and bring your attention to your body. Notice how deep or shallow your breath is at this moment. Notice how air is flowing past your nostrils as you inhale and exhale. Notice where the breath goes in your body — to your chest, your belly, or both. Relax your shoulders and neck (you can let your chin sink down to do this). Now begin to consciously draw in more air into your lungs. How does your energy and body change? Now notice your exhale. Is it much shorter than your inhale?

Now make a conscious effort to make it just as long as your inhale. You can count to four in your mind at the same pace to adjust your inhale and exhale to the same length. As a next step I'd like you to pause slightly at the moments between your inhale and exhale. Notice how that moment between the inhale and exhale holds special potential. Immerse yourself in this experience. Be completely present and aware of your body, your breath, and the practice at hand. Breathe deeply and slowly. When thoughts try to distract you, let them pass like leaves floating on a river. Don't attach them. Just notice them and let them go. Always return back to your breath. Keep going for at least five minutes.

You can set the timer on your cell phone to make sure you immerse yourself fully in this experience and don't distract your mind by wondering if the five minutes are up yet. Compare how you felt and how active your mind was before your breathing practice and after. What do you notice? Is your breath deeper now? Do you feel calm and relaxed? Did your mind relax as well? Do you feel more clear to make a decision that is not based on emotions of fleeting moment? Focusing on your breath can guide you to enter into your soul expanse and access the peace, clarity, and love of the present moment.

If you want to take it a step further, you can introduce mantras into your breath work or visualizations. For instance, on the inhale you could visualize that you are inhaling love and on the exhale you are releasing lower energies like stress from your body. Always notice how it makes you feel when you do this for a few minutes. I'm sure you will feel a deep shift in your energetic field — your state of being — your vibration will change drastically and when you are in that new state of being, new answers, new guidance, and new experiences aligned with source can surface into your awareness.

I've been taking this much time and effort to make meditation as easy and approachable for you as possible, because I know what a *huge* difference it can make for you. Just read through all the benefits again! But it's not only the scientifically proven facts that are relevant for me to help you establish this habit. My meditation practice has allowed me to access wisdom and healing beyond my human understanding.

I'm connecting with my Spirit Guides, Angels, Goddesses, Gods, Fairies, Celestials, and so many more light beings that have shared guidance, support, wisdom, and healing with me throughout the years. Now they are with me all the time and all it takes is to think of them.

This would not have been possible if I hadn't taken daily time to consciously connect, quiet my mind, and open myself up to higher spiritual wisdom and guidance. Truly, it has opened up countless new dimensions of being to me and the crazy thing is that I know there is still more to explore. It will never get boring. I'm a personal and spiritual growth junkie. If you're anything like me or if you simply feel the longing to understand the mysteries of life and *your* connection with it, I know the same is possible for you, if you choose to.

Tool #3

Chakra Clearing

Raise your Vibration

Level of difficulty: Intermediate

Time effort: Moderate

Frequency: Daily (ideally) or as often as your intuition tells you

Effects: Increases energy, raises your vibration, increases clarity, increases manifesting power by strengthening your energy signature, increases intuition, increases connection to source

Myths: Chakras are always equally strong. Chakras have little impact on you.

Goal: Clearing and strengthening your chakras so you reconnect with your soul and increase alignment with Spirit/God/Universe/Source to create flow in your life that leads to purpose, passion, fulfillment, and the rest of your soul's desires.

You may know the Sanskrit term chakra (energy center) from your yoga instructor. Yoga is a practice that is meant to strengthen your body, especially your spine, to sit in meditation with ease. Funny enough, I didn't know that until I was taught the philosophy behind yoga in the Yoga Teacher Training I attended in the Himalayas. Yoga also helps heal and strengthen the chakras, the energy centers, in your body. Yoga is a great practice to strengthen your body and mind, so if you feel called to indulge in it, do it. Here I'm going to share with you how you can consciously heal and strengthen your chakras through focused intention.

By now you know that you are 99.9 percent energy and only 0.1 percent matter. Your energy field is constantly fueled by your thoughts, beliefs, and emotions. It is your unique energy blueprint that consistently pulses out and interacts with the universal energy field that you and anything else in this Universe is part of. The frequency of your energy can be low vibrational or high vibrational. Thoughts of fear and hate are low vibrational and let your whole energy field pulse out low frequencies in the field. The opposite is true for thoughts and emotions of love or gratitude. The frequencies are high vibrational. Why is that important? The universal law of resonance will *always* bring to you experiences and people who are on your vibrational wavelength. If you are negative and consumed by hate, you will not go in resonance with joyful, happy and uplifting experiences. That's why happy people attract more happiness in their life. It's as if the Universe checks your energy and says, "Okay, she really likes to feel grateful, because that's what she does most of the time, so let's bring her more to be grateful for." What you hold consistently in your thoughts and heart will reflect in your outer experience.

Sometimes clients of mine worry that a bad thought or a feeling of being low for a couple of days will manifest negativity in their life and sabotage their positive manifestations. There is no need to worry though. We are not manifesting out of thin air in the third dimension. The Universe works itself from the creative plain of thought to the physical plain, where your desires manifest. This is a great security switch, because it gives you a time to adjust your energy and be at a different vibration once your manifestation rolls around.

What I find is that the higher your energy field vibrates, the faster your manifestations arrive. I can only explain it in the way that higher vibrations are pulsating faster and therefore attract faster results. While lower vibrations have a slower rate of impulse and are rather lethargic compared to positive vibes. The Universe also has a built-in drive to make an increase of life. So the closer you get to your high vibration, the more in tune you are with creation, with source, with your full creator power. Love is the energy that created this Universe. Only on earth we experience duality — love and hate, good and bad, high and low. We are on this planet to reconnect with our creator and with it reclaim our creator powers. Hate means destruction. Love means creation. Higher frequencies and positive thoughts *create* more life. Lower energies make us feel miserable because it goes against our Divine nature. Yet, often we choose to experience them to understand the polarity of light and darkness.

So, how can you raise your vibration so you manifest more rapidly and make an increase of life for the whole world?

You have seven chakras located in your body and a few more located above your crown chakra which are considered the spiritual chakras and an earth star below your feet. Chakras are energy centers that determine your energy field. A strong energy field is so beneficial on this journey of finding and living your soul purpose because the more powerful you are, the faster, clearer, and trusting you build your new life. The chakras can be vibrating and circulating freely or they can be blocked, which then also blocks your overall flow and well-being in life. Each chakra represents and strongly influences a certain area of your life.

Root Chakra
Position: Base of your spine
Color: Red
Represents: Grounding, Financial independence, Safety, Survival

Sacral Chakra
Position: Below navel
Color: Orange
Represents: Sexuality, Feminine energy, Nourishment, Receiving

Solar Plexus
Position: going up from the navel in waist line
Color: Yellow
Represents: Self-empowerment, Strength, Clarity, Stamina, Personal Power

Heart Chakra
Position: center of your chest
Color: Green
Represents: Love, Healing, Connection to all that is, Peace, Romance

Throat Chakra
Position: Throat
Color: Blue
Represents: Communication, Voicing your truth, Standing up for yourself

Third Eye
Position: slightly above and between the eyebrows
Color: Indigo blue
Represents: Clairvoyance, Intuitive knowing, Sight beyond the physical realm, Wisdom

Crown Chakra
Position: Top of the head
Color: Violet
Represents: Connection to the Divine, Spirituality, Bliss

Through our thoughts, behavior, and beliefs, our chakras can become clogged so they can no longer vibrate and circulate in their fullest function. When this happens, we experience this first as discomfort and then it manifests as illness in our physical bodies. But it can also show up as blockages in the correlated life areas. Our natural state is to have energy flowing to and from our energy centers, giving and receiving in abundance. Through limiting belief patterns, painful experiences, trauma, or even just our day-to-day encounters, our energy centers can be weakened or polluted.

That's why it is very beneficial to make chakra clearing a daily habit. But I suggest you start off with a routine that you feel comfortable committing to now. It will help you let go of energies that don't serve you regularly and don't build up residue that at some point will clog your energy field. This way you prevent feeling drained, "off," and you also don't lower your ability to manifest your desires with ease. You will feel more energy and clarity. Your manifesting abilities increase and you will experience flow in your life on a more consistent basis. The higher your vibration, the more clearly and faster you are communicating and cocreating with the Universe.

Chakra Clearing Practice:

Sit down on a chair and put your feet flat on the ground or sit cross-legged on a meditation pillow. Straighten your spine. Take a deep breath in, connect with your body and the present moment. Ground yourself by visualizing a cord or roots growing down into the core of the earth from the back of your spine and the soles of your feet. Draw her beautiful energy up into your body. Notice how it moves through your foot soles, up through your legs until it reaches your root chakra. Hold your attention right there and feel earth's pristine light replenish, clear, and strengthen your root chakra. Visualize that its beautiful red energy amplifies and grows.

When you feel ready, let light move further up to your sacral chakra. Hold your focus on the sacral chakra and set the intention that the earth's pristine healing light replenishes, clears, and strengthens the energy of your sacral chakra. Visualize a vivid orange color in its location and keep sending deeps breaths to reenergize your sacral chakra.

Keep moving like this through all of your chakras, one chakra up each time, until you reach your crown chakra. Hold your focus at each chakra, set the intention to clear and strengthen it, and visualize the corresponding color filling each one of your chakras. Keep breathing deeply and calmly. Notice the pristine light from the core of the earth flowing up through your chakras, energizing your whole body and aura. Take as much time as you need.

When you've cleansed your crown chakra, call upon the highest powers of love and light to send down crystalline white light from top to bottom through all your chakras. This time the energy is moving through your crown chakra first and then to your third eye, throat, heart, all the way down to your root chakra. With each breath, draw the crystalline light one chakra further down until all your chakras are flooded with the crystalline white light.

Now you are grounded into earth and connected to the heavens at the same time. Enjoy the feeling of being held in the energies of love and light. Your chakras are now fully cleansed. This is a beautiful state to conduct healing on yourself or to meditate.

If you'd like to go about your day, then please note: you have opened up your energy field very wide. When you go out and interact with the world in this way, it may feel disturbing and uncomfortable. You are energetically cracked open and energies will feel more intense.

So, I suggest that you conserve your high vibration by setting the intention to draw in your aura and close your chakras to a comfortable degree. You can set the intention to draw in your aura so that it ends with your body lines. I like to draw it in while inhaling. Additionally, you can close your chakras by visualizing them like blossoms that are closing into flower buds.

Tool #4

Cord Cutting

Releasing Draining Energies

Level of difficulty: Beginner

Time effort: Little

Frequency: Daily

Effects: Increases energy because draining cords from others have been cut, centering, reconnects you to *your* desires

Myths: Cutting cords means cutting people out of your life.

Goal: Recentering in your own energy, needs, and desires. Increasing your energy.

When I was first exposed to cord cutting, I was thrilled to have found a tool with which I can shake the sticky and uncomfortable feelings some interactions with people left on me. Do you sometimes meet people that for some inexplicable reason make you feel constricted and uncomfortable? And the feeling lingers throughout the rest of the day like a leech that keeps sucking the life out of you.

Or maybe you have people in your environment that are energy vampires. They feel on a high leaving after your chat over coffee, but you feel like all you need now is a good old nap to recharge your batteries. Often unconsciously, they latch on to your energy field and start fueling their own. It is a universal law though that a higher energy vibration will fuel a lower vibration energy, just like bodies of water will always balance out at one level when you join them. But the good news is, now that you know about this phenomena, you can manage it. You can decide who you stay with for a longer time and deliberately share your energy and who you'd rather not spend time with.

Cord Cutting #1: Preventing cords

Before you head in to meet that energy vampire friend of yours, you can set an intention that no cords may be attached to your energy field. If you believe and like the support of Angels (more on angels in the advanced section), you can ask Archangel Michael to protect you with his blue cloak. Intentions are powerful, because *you* are powerful. Take charge of your own energy!

Cord Cutting #2: Cutting cords

Take a moment and close your eyes. Place your feet flat on the ground and your hands palms facing upward on your thighs. Notice your breath and take a couple of deep breaths in and deep breaths out. Become centered in yourself and notice your energy. Notice where you feel expanded or constricted in your body. Where do you notice energy flowing freely and where does it seem to be inhibited? Notice where you feel energetic cords attached to your body. It can be in one of your chakras or it can be anywhere else. Even it is only in your aura, you'll feel a corresponding sensation in your body. And if you don't feel anything, this will still work.

You'll smile at how easy this is — energy work is really easy. The reason why it often doesn't "work" is that the intention is not strong enough. You don't trust that it's done. So, here's what you'll do: set the intention that right now, in this moment, all cords that are not made of love and light are being cut through all dimensions of time and space. Boom. That's it. If you like a bit of angel flavor with this one too, then ask Archangel Michael to do it for you. Angels are incredibly helpful and omnipresent expression of the Divine source. They will ALWAYS help you. So if you don't trust your own power enough right now, take a shortcut and ask them to do it.

Then notice how your energy changes. Notice that where energy seemed to stall, it starts flowing again. Maybe you can even feel the cords undocking or falling off you. See how they are transmuting back to love and light.

The next step is to replenish these areas in your aura (energy field) by sending healing to you and the other people where the cords have just been cut. You can pray for this by saying silently or out loud: "Thank you for replenishing and strengthening my aura and the auras of all other involved people. I am healed. I am whole. And so it is."

Tool #5

Surrender and Acceptance

Flow with Life

Level of difficulty: Beginner

Time effort: Little

Frequency: Ongoing

Effects: Increases trust in the universal flow of life, detaches from the outcome, surrenders to a higher wisdom, opens up for new solutions, increases joy and zest for life

Myths: Surrender means giving up. Not being in control means not receiving what you desire. Surrender means not taking any more action.

Goal: Opening yourself up for miracles. Letting go of control and welcoming a higher wisdom (from your higher self, your soul) so that you can be guided in a direction that truly supports you, accepting the present moment to create a better future, letting go of attachments to let new and better experiences enter

Often times, we argue with reality because from our human perception, we believe it should be different. Often we don't even know in which way we want it to be different, but we dwell so much on what others seem to have and we don't, that we forget to be fully present in our own lives. Every experience you have in your life is a result of your past thinking and the actions you took based on that. It is a mirror of your evolution and shows you exactly what needs to be healed, released, and acknowledged so that you can reach your next level of happiness, abundance, or health.

You are the creator of all the experiences you have in your life and they don't happen to you randomly. Sometimes it can be challenging to accept that on some karmic or subconscious level, we have brought painful experiences into our lives. But in Divine truth, no experience is good or bad. It just is. Good or bad only exists in our dualistic world where we need to label everything to make sense of it for the sake of our mind's sanity.

"Life will give you whatever experience is most helpful for the evolution of your consciousness. How do you know this is the experience you need? Because this is the experience you are having at the moment."
– Eckhart Tolle

When you think back over your life, did you ever have an experience that you labeled "bad" in the moment you were in it, yet looking back you see it rather as a blessing in disguise? Take a moment and really think about it. Come up with one or even more experiences like that. Maybe you remember a breakup with a partner that was painful, but ultimately paved the way for an even more loving relationship. Or maybe you lost a job and although it was hard in that moment, you were actually redirected to a job that was more fulfilling or a true stepping stone for you. When you are able to accept the experiences you have in your life for what they really are — mirrors of self-development — you start shifting your focus and perspective on them.

You can start by asking, "How does this situation serve me?" "What can I learn from this situation?" "What is my part in creating this situation?" When you fully accept what is happening in your life, as it is happening *for* you instead of *to* you, you are opening yourself up to your Divine guidance and enter the reality of the miracle-minded person. You surrender to what is and transcend your reality instead of resisting the lesson, healing, and energetic upleveling that wants to happen for and through you.

Byron Katie said, "Every time I argue with reality, I lose." This sentence has stuck with me over years. It boils down in such simplicity that you can never win when you resist the infinite intelligence of the Universe that wants to work through you and with you so that you can realize and reclaim your role as a skilled creator. When you block yourself to grow from a situation and step into full responsibility, you are making yourself the victim. Victims have no power. Victims believe they have no control over their own fate and they suffer, for they believe there is nothing they can do to create change. It's not true. Everyone is created equal. We are all part of the one spirit and we all have the power to create lasting change in our lives.

But first we need to accept where we are fully, take responsibility, and consciously make new choices. We so often fail to fully accept what we have created because it is painful. It's painful to accept that we may have made a mistake or that we may have detoured from our purpose. The Universe is self-correctional. The mistake you think you made was not a mistake, it was the Universe directing you toward your higher good.

And sometimes we have to go really far into the opposite direction of happiness and fulfillment, so that we can realize what we *don't* want. The faster you can accept and transcend the situation by changing your point of view and asking better questions, the sooner you recenter in the now, reconnect to your full power that lies in that moment and invite healing, clarity, and growth. This way you release yourself from the burden of judging your experience and wishing it to be different and instead invite spirit in to lift you to your next level experience.

Exercise:

- Is there any area of your life that you have been struggling to accept fully into your experience? Take out your journal and describe it. Why have you been resisting to feel it?

- What aspects of this experience have you been focusing on? What meaning have you given this situation? Have you been playing the part of the victim or the perpetrator?

- In which way would you need to shift your perception to begin seeing the situation as a blessing in disguise for you and anybody else involved? Take a moment and sit in silence. Ask your higher self and spirit to give you answers and help you shift your perspective to see love instead of fear in this situation, so that you may no longer buy into the false perceptions of the physical world, but that your mind be elevated to the planes of Divine truth.

Tool #6

Gratitude

Relate to Source in Harmony

Level of difficulty: Beginner

Time effort: Little

Frequency: Ongoing + Daily

Effects: Changes your perspective to recognize abundance in your life. Lets the Universe bring more of what you desire to you. Relates your energy to the Supreme so that you can communicate more clearly.

Myths: Gratitude and positivity are airy new age concepts.

Goal: Shifting your perspective to abundance. Training your focus to notice what you desire more of in your life. Giving the Universe clear instruction on what you want in your life so it can deliver accordingly. Creating a harmonic energy between you and the Divine.

Where attention goes, energy flows. It's that simple. When you notice everything that you feel grateful for in your life, the Universe listens. It basically makes the connection that you seem to want to have more to be grateful for, because that's where you dwell most of the time. This is also called the Law of Attraction or Law of Resonance. Your thoughts aren't private.

Your thoughts are part of all of creation and you communicate with the universal field that you're part of with every thought you think. Your thought influences your energy signature and your energy signature draws back from the field what matches (goes in resonance) with that thought. That's why self-fulfilling prophecies work and why you always get more of what you consistently focus on. Focus on lack and you'll get more of that. Focus on how you're being treated unfairly and you'll get more of that.

Our mind loves to work in the same way we have conditioned it. Mindset work takes conscious effort. We need to retrain ourselves to not fall into the trap of unhealthy thought processes. The easiest way to refocus and retrain ourselves *and* to change our life for the better is to practice gratitude.

Practice #1: Gratitude Journal

Don't go straight into brushing this off the table. I'm sure you've heard this before and maybe you're not particularly fond of the idea. I don't know. But let me explain why it's powerful and how to use it *right*.

A gratitude journal is so powerful because it asks you to think of your day in a completely different way. It prompts you to look past the things that may not have gone well and find things, experiences, or people that you're thankful for. It can be small or big. But what it does is shift your perspective to see the good. Remember the Wayne Dyer quote? "Loving people live in a loving world. Hostile people live in a hostile world. Same world." There is beauty, grace, and positivity in every day. Whether you choose to acknowledge it or not. And there will always be things that don't go as we'd like them to. That's okay. The difference in your energy and happiness is what you choose to focus on and what meaning you give it.

For instance, if you focus on how you're being passed over for a promotion and for you that means that you're not good enough. How does it make you feel? What if you could radically shift this thought and invite a miracle-minded approach to seeing this: "I was passed over because this wasn't to my highest good, although I thought it would be, and the Universe is preparing something even better for me that will bring me long-term fulfillment. I am open to receive." How does that make you feel? Umm, very different I would guess.

Life happens FOR you, not TO you.

How to use your journal:

If you'd like to have a physical journal that you can carry with you or leave by your bedside, then get one that you really love looking at, feeling in your hand, and carrying with you. Treat yourself! If you're more a techie, then use your Evernote and create a brand new notebook.

Every evening before going to bed you'll write down at least five things, people, and experiences you are grateful for.

Only choose to write down what you feel an emotion for. You're not keeping this journal because you have too much time, but because you're following a goal. The goal is to put you in the frequency/vibration/energy of gratitude. You will only get there when you can *FEEL* grateful for what you're writing in that very moment. If it has no emotional charge, then modify it or find something else. It'll get easier the more you do it. Train that muscle, baby!

It helps to be very detailed in order to find the emotional charge. Often, "I am thankful the sun was shining" has little to no emotional charge. Instead, "I'm so grateful for the way the old man smiled at me on the street for no apparent reason. He seemed so happy and I'm glad I was there in that moment when he shared a bit of his happiness with me," has a lot of emotional charge. The more depth and detail you give it, the more it will resonate with your soul in gratitude.

Make, "I'm thankful for baking a delicious cake" more powerful by adding details like, "I'm thankful that the cake I baked turned out delicious. The dough was just as I wanted it to be, I grated the apples safely and still have all my fingertips, and everyone who tried it loved it so much. They even asked for seconds and I could see it was a highlight in their day. I rejoice in the happiness I could share with this simple cake." See what I mean?

Don't name the same thing twice.

Always find something new, every single day!

"I have noticed that the Universe loves Gratitude.
The more Grateful you are, the more goodies you get."
– Louise Hay

Practice #2: Gratitude Walk

I walk my dog Mojo during lunch time every day. Often I listen to podcasts or audio trainings, but sometimes I make it a gratitude walk. All the way, I will find things in my life that I'm grateful for. I'll allow the soft, warm feeling to spread from my heart chakra into my whole body. It's amazing what an hour of gratitude can do for you.

I always feel motivated, recharged, and ready to head into the afternoon. You can also do this on your commute to work, while exercising at the gym, or waiting for a friend. Instead of reading useless posts on social media, use the time to let the Universe know what you'd like more of and raise your vibration so that you're a match to receive it.

Try it out!

Tool #7

Prayer

Communicate with Source

Level of difficulty: Beginner

Time effort: Little

Frequency: on demand

Effects: Lets you communicate your hopes, dreams, desires, and worries to the Universe, so that the Universe can step in and help you.

Myths: You need to steadily pray for what you desire.

Goal: Receive Divine intervention, guidance and support.

Fun fact: most people *don't* know how to pray. Prayer does not mean repeating the same string of words over and over. Many do this and wonder why their request is not getting heard. Well, first of all, if you keep asking for what you want, you are resetting the delivery status to "order placed." It can never reach you.

Second, people formulate their prayers in the form of lack. For instance, "Dear God, please send me money." It states the lack of money and emphasizes that you seem to be unable to do something about it. What about: "Dear God, thank you for sending me 100 dollars by Friday and for clearly highlighting to me through which channel I can best receive it. And so it is. I'm so grateful." Feels different, doesn't it? God can get on board with the second prayer, because you are taking responsibility to cocreate with him.

It's like that scene in *Hitch – The Date Doctor* where he explains to Albert Brennaman that you never go all the way to get the kiss. You go ninety percent and the women leans in the last ten percent. Same with the Universe. The Universe is a gentleman who will never come 100 percent to land a juicy smooch on your lips. It honors your creator powers and free will (just like Hitch) and lets you decide whether you are willing to receive what it has to offer. Getting up and opening the door to receive your package is an act too, you know. And while you're at the door, you can still decide whether to receive or decline. Just like taking the last ten percent to get the kiss.

Wallace Wattles explains it well when he says, "You do not make this impression [communicate your desires to source] by repeating strings of words; In order to get rich [or whatever else you desire] you need to pray without ceasing. And by prayer I mean holding steadily to your *vision*, with the *purpose* to cause its creation into solid form, and the *faith* that you are doing so." What Wattles says here is that first of all you need to be 100 percent clear about what you desire — that's your vision. Then you go about creating that in full faith that the Universe has already heard you and is conspiring to help you to make it happen. That's how a person who is rooted in her essence, power, and potential manifests.

Exercise:

Create your vision of what your purposeful life looks like for you. Make it very tangible and add every important detail. This will help you to stay en route to your desired destination. Now move ahead with the purpose to reach your goal and the faith that it is already yours. All you need to do is draw the potential from the infinite universal field.

Tool #8

Intention

Create with clear purpose

Level of difficulty: Beginner

Time effort: Little

Frequency: On demand

Effects: Steers you and the Universe purposefully to the creation of your desires.

Myths: Intention is unnecessary.

Goal: Clarifying your vision and desires so that you and the Universe can fully align with your goals.

Intentions are among the most potent tools. Although they are so easy to use, they make all the difference on your path. Lack of intention can lead to failure, just as well as not being aware of the intentions you are carrying.

Intention is best given to the Supreme through harmonious alignment, speak — an open heart. Attune yourself to spirit to hand over your intentions with the highest potency.

Let's say you are having a meeting with a couple of people from your company. What's the first thing you do to make it a success? You ask yourself what you desire as an outcome, right? You get the people in the room and you consciously steer them in the direction of your preferred outcome. Maybe you've prepared slides, data, or reports that support your case. You convince your colleagues and leave with your desired outcome. Basically, you've set a very clear intention on what your desired outcome is. You've selected the right people to invite, you've selected the information to support your case, and you've showed up with purpose. It's a success.

But haven't we all been in meetings that had no intention, direction, or desired outcome? They are messy, undirected, and often leave everyone feeling like they just wasted an hour of their life for no outcome at all.

Intention is everything. It gives clear direction and purpose to everything you do. Seeing clear intentions in every interaction, goal, and relationship lets you take the steering wheel of your life and will prevent many unnecessary detours.

How it works:

You can imagine intention like a program that you activate in your energy field. Once planted, the program starts running and begins to draw experiences, messages, and people from the universal field that resonate with it.

It will also show you what mindset patterns and wounds clash with the running program and need to be released so that it can continue to run smoothly and bring you your desired outcome. It's the speedway to getting exactly what you want.

An intention sets you on a clear and purposeful path, so make sure you're aware of the intentions you set.

Here is some inspiration on how you can use intention:

- **Healing:** If you carry a trauma, habit, or wound that you'd like to heal, use intention as a way to be guided to the right healing path. For instance, you can say, "My intention is to let go of xyz in Divine timing in a way that fully supports my highest good. I'd like the healing journey to be gracious, pleasant, and uplifting."

- **Mindset:** If you realized there are limiting belief systems that you're ready to let go of, make it known and plant the seed in your energy field through intention. Be aware of the interactions and insights that you have from that point onward, which will show you a different perspective. It may be something you read, hear, or experience. The Universe will always give you colorful support; your job is to be open to receive the lesson and healing.

- **Success:** One of my favorite ways to use intentions is to move myself closer toward my goals. Let's say I set the intention to let go of any blocks (mindset, energy, etc.) that are standing in the way of achieving goal xyz. It's so easy, because once the intention is set, I know the Universe will present all the blocks and all I need to do is to release them.

- **Purpose:** Just a few pages ago, we set the intention that you will find your life purpose. But you can set more intentions connected to your purpose as you move along. Check back at where you are on your path, where you may feel stuck or confused. You can always set an intention to resolve any situation by finding the best possible solution for everyone involved. Once you plant the seed in your energy field, it will pull you forward.

Intention Practice:

- Put intentions to the test: Go meet a friend with no intention vs. meeting a friend with a clear intention (have fun, support, uplift, console, or a combination of many). Note in which way you experienced the meetings differently.

- Try it: choose one of the scenarios above (or create your own) and set a clear intention. Make your new intentions known to the Universe! And remember, thinking it is enough, the Universe knows you inside out.

Tool #9

Connecting to Spirit Realm

Receive Personalized Guidance

Level of difficulty: Advanced

Time effort: Medium

Frequency: Ongoing + Daily

Effects: Transcends your current reality. Increases clarity and direction.

Myths: Angels and other light beings aren't real.

Goal: Receiving personalized guidance about your life path and goals. Clearer than the conceptual guidance you receive through intuition.

I'm such a big fan of connecting to the spirit realm. The beings of the highest powers of love and light are always eager to help and support you. They are benevolent advisors, wise counselors, powerful healers, and incredible magicians. You will find that you feel more drawn to some of them than others because you may need their light and knowledge more at this point.

Many of the light beings I connect with have become friends. This may sound weird if you haven't had a lot of contact yet, but it's possible for you too. You're never alone and have powerful friends with you, who support and guide you. Oh, and yes, feeling their energy is soothing and strong, but they have their own characters. The more you open up to them and connect with them, you'll see that they have humor or speak very directly. They energies are very different, because they represent different archetypes of energy.

Over the years I've worked with many light beings from Angels, to Gods/Goddesses, Ascended Masters, and Fairies. I believe Angels are the easiest ones to start out with when you're recalibrating your skills. They are expressions of love and light that are at your service. All light beings are omnipresent, which means that they can be with you and everybody else on the planet at the same time. They are from another dimension where time and space do not exist in this linear way as we experience it. They are always eager to help you, but you need to ask them for their support. They won't help unless you ask, because they respect your free will choices.

When I started training my psychic senses and connection to the spirit realm, I drew an Angel Oracle Card every day. I would make an appointment with them like you would when you'd meet a friend. They really love to see your commitment.

Sometimes I get asked about dark energies and opening up to the wrong type of guidance. You're on the safe side when you make it known who you are connecting with. You have the power! Whenever I tune in, I always say that I'm connecting with or drawing energy and healing from the "Highest Powers of Love and Light." You can add, "all others I bind from me" if that makes you feel better.

If you feel this is something you'd like to explore further, go ahead and try the practices I provide here. It is fantastic to get guidance from your higher self, angels, or any other light being you connect to. It does take practice to get the messages clear. In the beginning, it may be difficult to differentiate your ego from your higher self-guidance.

Tip: Ask Archangel Michael to babysit your ego while you're connected. Ask him to take it shopping or whatever other activity would keep it really busy and engaged, so that you are free from ego distractions. Sometimes you may need to send it away more than once. That's okay, some days it's more active than other days.

Practice #1: Oracle Cards

I used Doreen Virtue's Oracle Card sets to connect to specific light beings and learn about them, but also to get guidance on my next steps. Her cards are very positive and helpful. There are many other card decks out there, but I find her card decks have a high vibration that I resonate with. You can go to Amazon or the app store and follow your intuition on which one is aligned with you right now.

I'd recommend you start out connecting with angels, because they are so high-frequential and clear. Get a card deck that features different Archangels or Angels. Make an appointment with your angels for the same time every day. Have a sacred space created, be on time, grounded, tuned in, and ready to communicate. Set an intention and pray over the cards: Thank you for letting me pick exactly that card that will show me the angel whose essence most supports my highest good today. You can learn more about how to use the cards by reading the instructions that come with it. When you have your card, call upon the Angel. A thought is enough. Notice how the energy around you changes. Notice the quality of the energy. Notice any thoughts that pop in your head. You may have visions, feelings, or knowing. Trust that what you perceive is the angel connecting with you through your intuition. You may even see the color of the angel. In the beginning, the encounters may be vague, but if you keep practicing it will get clearer and clearer.

I know many go into this practice with the deep desire to see an angel. We humans often believe that a real life apparition is the only real deal. It's not true. I was craving the same when I started reconnecting with my psychic gifts. After a while, I had already put the thought aside that I needed to see an angel with my physical eyes, and Archangel Raziel appeared in front of me. Not a physical eye apparition, but boy was I blown away. I saw him with my spiritual vision through a vision, standing at the foot of my bed. He was majestic and filled the whole room. His energy was so...mighty, clear, and all encompassing. Remembering this moment still gives me goosebumps. He showed himself to me in his bigger energetic form (probably still not the whole essence of who he is), as much as I could take in that moment. I wouldn't have been ready for an angel to manifest in front of me. I was already intimidated by what he showed me that day. I remember thinking, "Wow, these are the energies I work with." It was a glimpse into the full might of the Divine.

Your experiences will most likely be different. They'll be unique to you and what you need to experience on your path. The veil to the other side is getting thinner and we are ascending into a higher frequency. This makes it easier to access higher knowledge and to connect with light beings. If you feel this is for you, trust that you'll experience all you need in that moment. Keep showing up. The spirit realm loves commitment.

Practice #2: Meditation

Another way to connect with the spirit realm is to ask them into your meditation. You can address one light being directly to support you with a certain topic or you can leave it open and ask for support in general. Pay attention to your vision, feelings, body sensations, and your intuitive knowing, because that's how they will communicate with you. They speak to you in conceptual, intuitive ways. It takes some training to understand and trust the messages, but you'll get the hang of it the more often you do it.

If you'd like to meditate with light beings, but don't know how yet, I channel energetically charged meditations with high vibing light beings over on my website: sharonkirstin.com

Practice #3: Automatic Writing

Bust out your journal and let's give this a try. As I was starting out, automatic writing was my absolute favorite way of getting crystal clear guidance from my spiritual buddies on the other side. It never get's old and I still use it regularly.

You basically open yourself up to let Spirit move your hand and write down the answers to your questions.

This is how it works:

- Create your sacred space: no distractions or disturbances, music if you like, candles to create an atmosphere, and invite in the Divine spark

- Ground yourself, clear your energy field (chakras), and connect to the highest powers of love and light

- Send the Ego to go babysitting with Archangel Michael

- Have a journal or blank sheets of paper in front of you

- Always start out by addressing who you're asking to receive guidance from, for instance, "Dear God / Dear Archangel Michael / Dear Higher Self / Dear Spirit Guides / Dear Highest Powers of Love and Light"

- Then state the topic you'd like guidance on, "I've been confused/worried/etc. about xyz…" You can go as short or long as you wish. Not that it makes a difference to who you're talking to (because they know you), but it can be cathartic and clarifying for you.

- Then ask them for answers, "…Please tell me exactly what the next best steps are for me to achieve xyz. Thank you," or something similar.

- This is where the magic happens: Turn off your head and write down whatever pops in your mind. You may hear it word for word or your hand may just start writing. Anything can happen. Just go with the flow.

- Sometimes we get too nervous and block the flow. In this case: send the ego away again and begin by writing, "I don't know what to write." Over and over again until something new shows up. The repetition will help turn off your mind and let go of expectations.

- Keep practicing. The more you do it, the easier and clearer your answers will become.

Tool #10

Visualization

Imprint your Desire into the Field to Create its Form

Level of difficulty: Intermediate

Time effort: Medium

Frequency: Ongoing + Daily

Effects: Manifest your desires.

Myths: Your mind is separate from source.

Goal: Giving a clear mental picture to Source Energy/the Universe to create from thought form into physical form.

When you're acting from your Divine essence you are drawing on the powers of creation to get what you desire. You are *never* in competition for what has already been created, because you know the Universe is infinitely abundant and there is more than enough for everyone.

You create, not compete.

To create from the formless substance of the quantum energy field, you need to create a clear mental picture of what you desire. You imprint your desire onto the field through visualization. What you continuously see, charged with positive emotion, will be drawn onto the physical plane of creation, so that it can reach you. Your energy signature communicates with the field and causes the creation and attraction through the physical channels.

It's important that you hold steady to your vision with the *purpose* to have it created and the *faith* that it is already yours. It is already on its way to you; there is only a small lag time between impressing the vision as thought onto the field and receiving it back on the physical plane. What you desire does not suddenly appear miraculously, but it will come to you through the already existing channels of commerce.

You will need to act with purpose to receive your vision and you will need to stay attuned to source through gratitude so that you will know which actions to take. You can speed up the creation of your desires by increasing your faith, holding steady to your purpose with action and staying in harmony to receive through gratitude.

Visualization Practice:

- Create a mental picture of your desired life. Be very specific with the details. The details are what will motivate you to keep focused and going. The details create the emotional charge for you.

- Create a vision board with all the details of your desired life. Look at it every day and place it in a spot where you will subconsciously be exposed to it. Screensavers, opposite your desk, anything goes.

- Practice gratitude that your desires are already yours. Attune yourself to Spirit through gratitude for everything you already have. In this state of intense gratitude, visualize your desires manifested. This will speed up the creation of your desires. Do it daily!

- Be aware of your decisions and actions. Do they lead you closer to your desired life? When you've planted your vision in your heart and have full purpose to reach it, you'll automatically be taking actions that will lead you closer to your desired life. That's why it is important to have a clear vision and to imprint it on your subconscious and with it on the quantum field that you are part of.

Crafting Your Spiritual Attunement Practice

Knowing the ten tools is not enough. You need to put them into practice. Knowledge without action is useless.

> *"Without knowledge action is useless and*
> *knowledge without action is futile."*
> *— Abu Bakr*

In your exclusive and free workbook, I help you create your own daily practice and keep track of your progress. It's easy to be motivated for a week and then drop off the wagon.

Your desired life of purpose will manifest if you show up consistently with intention. I've created a daily planner that will help you stay on your purposeful track. Download here: sharonkirstin.com/bookbonus

Morning Practice: (15 minutes)

- Grounding (1 minute)
    - Creates a safe space
    - Activates your energy flow
- Gratitude (5 minutes)
    - Attunes you to source, so that you're in harmony with your essence.
    - Puts you in a state to communicate your desires to Spirit
- Intention: (2 minutes)
    - Be clear on how you'd like the day to be, who will you be, what will you do, state what would make today great
- Visualization: (5 minutes)
    - Hand your desires over to Spirit through clear visions and emotions
    - See and feel your daily goals, three-month goals and six-month goals as manifested.
    - Own them as already yours and give thanks.

During the day:

- Mindfulness: Be aware of your actions and reactions to find energy and mindset blocks that may still block your flow.
- Mindset: Speak positive affirmations and own your alter-ego energy.
- Intentions: Be intentional in all your actions.
- Inspired action: Take action that will lead you closer to your purpose and dreams.

Evening Practice: (~21 minutes)

- Cord Cutting: (1 minute)
    - Detaches energy leaks from cords that are not made of love and light
    - Heals you and the other person
- Chakra Clearing: (5 – 10 minutes)
    - Increases the energy flow in your body, aura, and chakras
    - Deep healing effect
    - Increases the vibration of your electromagnetic field and with it your manifestation powers
- Meditation: (10 minutes – open end)
    - Surrender to Spirit
    - Silent meditation or mantra meditation
    - Effect: Rejuvenating, stress reduction, increases inner peace
    - Meditation Journeys with the spirit realm
    - Effect: Healing and guiding

Transforming a Personal Topic:

If you have a topic you'd like targeted support from Spirit, these practices will help you transcend your current challenges and ascend into a higher vibration. For best results, set aside an hour in the evening to dedicate to this healing process. Go through all the outlined steps below.

1. **Grounding**: Plug into Mother Earth for additional support to easily transmute heavy energies and receive healing.
2. **Gratitude**: Relate yourself to Spirit in harmony and open your heart to communicate.
3. **Prayer**: Give all worries and cares to Spirit.
4. **Surrender**: Let go and place your topic in the hands of the Supreme.
5. **Faith**: Trust that it has been heard and you're already receiving help.
6. **Intention**: State crystal clearly what you desire. How do you want to feel? How do you want the healing process to be?
7. **Cord Cutting**: Cut all cords to the past concerning this situation.
8. **Chakra Cleanse**: Clear everything (mindset, energy, karma, past lives) connected to this topic out of your energy field.
9. **Meditation**: Sit in silence, receive healing energies, and let Spirit show you visions and guidance related to your topic.

10. **Automatic Writing (optional):** If you're looking for more guidance and information.

11. **Rest (optional):** Spirit can best heal you if you step aside and let them take care of it.

12. **Inspired Action:** Act, based on the guidance you received when you feel the timing is right.

Summary Step #6:

- When you're attuned to Spirit, the Infinite Intelligence of the Universe, you receive accurate guidance.

- Since you are part of the Universe, your creator knows you. The Supreme knows your mind, hears your intentions, worries, and concerns. It always wants the best for you and supports you endlessly in magical ways.

- What you will receive as an answer, is intuition in you on how to do it.

- You can attune yourself to understand this intuitive, conceptual language of Spirit, just like you can learn any human language.

- When you align in harmony with Spirit, your spidey senses peak and you feel like your intuition is on fire. You have an inner compass that is guiding you to your highest fulfillment.

- Being tuned into Spirit is our most natural state of being. Nothing needs to be added to tap into source; it's rather a dropping of all unnecessary concepts.

- Our aspirations and desires are a sign of the Divine pulsing through our veins and energy field. Every aspect of who we are is Divine perfection.

- We are not only human, we are a soul as well. Just because we're having a human experience, it doesn't mean that all the higher knowledge is gone. It's in storage so we can fully be present in the human experience we're having right now.

- The mind will automatically go to negativity if we do not actively train it to interpret things in a more constructive, positive way.

- Learn the ten tools that help you cultivate a strong connection to the very source of who you are, so that you are aligned with source energy in harmony.

- Attuned to your soul essence (source energy, Spirit, the Supreme) in complete harmony, you receive crystal clear guidance on what your purpose is and how to best manifest it in your life.

- Above that it also reconnects you to your psychic powers of clairvoyance, clairsentience, claircognizance, etc. Your intuition will be on fire!

- Learn how to create your personalized daily routine to master your intuition, spirit guidance, and higher spiritual knowledge.

- Download the free workbook at sharonkirstin.com/bookbonus

Conclusion & Next Steps

"Why do you stay in prison when the door is so wide open?"
— Rumi

The mere fact that you are thinking about a purposeful life, and you're holding this book in your hands, means that you are *called to fulfill your purpose.* The knowledge in this book will serve you greatly to find your path, power and purpose, if you do the work and follow the steps.

You have unique talents and gifts that are intentionally part of your essence so that you can serve a purposeful role in this world.

No matter how far you have detoured from your happiness, purpose or potential, there is always a path to reconnect to your soul's truth. I have outlined a total of six necessary steps to purpose with many self-inquiry exercises and spiritual practices so you can step into your power.

The clarity with which you can see and live your purpose is decreased by mindset, ego, and belief-systems that create layers of distortion. This makes it is harder for you to communicate clearly with your soul essence and Spirit. These layers can be peeled through radical self-awareness.

You are a soul having a human experience. Your soul is part of the Infinite Intelligence of the Universe. It *is* the Universe. You are part of the quantum field that is the Universe because you are made up of 99.9 percent energy that constantly interacts with the field through electromagnetic impulses that attract experiences, people and things from the universal field.

This makes you an active and limitlessly powerful cocreator with the essence of all of life. You are never separated. Your thoughts and emotions are never private, but cause a reaction that always travels back to you.

Source or Spirit guides you in intuitive, conceptual ways. You can learn to understand it's language just like you can learn any human language. You do this by attuning yourself in harmony to source energy. I have introduced you to ten spiritual tools and how to use them in your everyday life.

What to do NOW

Never leave the site of a decision without taking immediate action. That's what Tony Robbins preaches to his students and it has definitely fallen on fertile ground in my mind. Knowledge without action is worth absolutely nothing. You can know everything in this world that there is to know about anything, but if you don't put in the work to create it, you have nothing. The knowledge needs to be seeded into action. This is the only recipe that will give you real results.

Reading a book is great and soaking up new concepts is great. Maybe even being inspired by them is great, too. But what will it be worth in your life? There is no magic bullet that will transform your life into its best version without you having to put in the work.

What can you do to motivate yourself to take immediate action? Find the pain in the current situation and make it bigger than the pleasure you get from it!

One thing is almost certain — you're heading in a direction in your life that you do not enjoy, that makes you feel pain. Maybe you hate going to work, maybe you feel uninspired, maybe you have health issues. Something is going on that made you pick up this book.

What does it take to create your own destination in life? Your own vision of success, abundance, fulfillment, and purpose? You'd have to walk a different path from the masses. Maybe one that has never been walked before. You wouldn't even see the whole path most of the time. The outcome may be uncertain at times. The pain of getting out of your comfort zone and creating a new destination requires effort, stamina, vision, faith, and persistence.

What do most people do when faced with this decision?

Surprising, but...absolutely *nothing*.

Why would anybody keep walking toward the cliff?! The fall, pain, failure, and frustration are apparent. People keep walking toward the deadly cliff because it is comfortable. Other people are walking with you. You're not alone. You're swimming with the current. The path is paved with comfort, drama, and lots of entertainment to keep the gaze and focus off the imminent doom. If they just looked up for a moment toward their destination and became conscious of where they're going, they'd see that they'll sooner or later fall to death. But they don't dare to look up. They're hypnotized by mass media and society to not question what they're told.

They keep walking toward the cliff, because staying on course doesn't require any (uncomfortable) action *right now*.

> *"In every moment there's the possibility of a better future, but you people won't believe it. And because you won't believe it you won't do what is necessary to make it a reality. So, you dwell on this terrible future. You resign yourselves to it for one reason, because *that* future does not ask anything of you today."*
>
> *– Nix, Tomorrowland*

Your next steps:

- Download the free workbook at sharonkirstin.com/bookbonus
- Visit sharonkirstin.com and sign up for the free Purpose Video Course
- Check out the transformational meditations and courses I have created for you
- Want to work with me personally to help you transform into your best version and live a life on purpose? Learn more here: sharonkirstin.com

Whatever you do, just don't close the book and do nothing. Don't leave the site of reading this book without taking action! Action will change your life for the better. Procrastination won't.

Your Wake-Up Call

Remember what I told you about Sam? He could've watched my Youtube video on how a life falling apart is a good thing and just leave it at that. But what created real and lasting change for him was that he took action. He followed his inner guidance and reached out to me.

If he had just moved on to the next video and looked for more knowledge, nothing would've changed. He would have more and more information on his situation and how he's stuck, but he wouldn't have moved transcended and resolved that situation at all.

Instead he chose to see it as a sign that he felt a connection to my words and energy. With this faith, he changed the course of his destiny within a few short weeks. He's a different man now who operates from a place of intuition and personal power. He was willing to dig up the pain from the past so that it could dissolve in the light of awareness and healing. His soul was ready for transformation and he was guided to fulfill his purpose. All he needed was a mentor who could crack him open to his essence and his raw truth. I know it wasn't always easy for him to look at his own disempowering concepts, fears, and beliefs — it isn't for any of my clients, including myself. It can be scary to challenge everything you've come to believe about yourself. But that's all it is.

Just a belief. It's not the truth. Realigning back with your authentic self is a homecoming, a relief, and creates a sense of deep peace.

Yes, action and change may seem scary in the beginning. The ego tries to talk you out of it. But I've never heard anybody say, "Gosh, I wish I hadn't challenged myself to be a better version of myself. I'd be so much happier living unconsciously."

If you hear the call to wake up, it's time to listen.

It's special. Not everybody hears it.

You're chosen to rise up and become more of who you really are at the core of your being.

This call is just for you. It's here to wake you up to purpose, potential, and fulfillment.

Ready? Wake up!

About the Author

Sharon Kirstin is an author, coach, healer, and spiritual teacher. She is a breakthrough artist who takes her clients from stuck to buzzing in record time. With her psychic gifts, she helps you transcend the three-dimensional view of life and opens your awareness to mystical dimensions of existence. She initiates you to realign with your soul's true essence, wisdom, and power. Reattuned to your cosmic life force, you are ready to create an authentic and successful life on your own terms, independent of society's expectations. You have the potential to make a bigger impact by expressing your soul's purpose in life and business. Own it! It's time.

Sharon left her corporate career as a Director for a Fashion E-commerce company to follow her soul's call to higher purpose. She holds a double degree in International Business Administration from German and American Universities and three levels of Life Coaching degrees from internationally renowned spiritual mentor Isabelle von Fallois. Her psychic gifts, accurate guidance, and transformational healings are praised by the beautiful testimonials from her clients. She loves to share the wisdom and energy Spirit channels through her in various forms like books, courses, meditations, healings, group, and client sessions.

You can reach her and learn more about her work here: sharonkirstin.com